THE SILENT PATH

Avi

ISBN: 9780578637068

For permission requests, contact
Nirvana Foundation
Email: info@nirvana.foundation
Website: www.nirvana.foundation

The whole universe has to come together to move a single blade of grass. This book would not have been possible without the support of everything that has ever happened.

The Silent Path

CONTENTS

The Silent Path

Foreword

The Silent Path: Awaken to Your Highest Possibility provides the perfect introduction to meditation for newcomers to the practice. It speaks about cultivating individuality and purpose in life against the onslaught of collective thinking pressures.

Avi points out that few modern systems "are working for the liberation of the individual." Most are juggernauts of collective melding that work for themselves. This is why meditation can provide answers that society cannot. It's individual-centric, and just as society cares little about inner pursuits, so the foundation question "Who am I" cannot be addressed by society, but marks a path of self-inquiry that meditation supports.

Those who embark on this journey will realize new possibilities, from renewed purpose and identity to revised approaches to life itself. And that's what The Silent Path is all about.

Readers already contemplating a personal journey towards enlightenment will find The Silent Path intriguing in many ways. For one, it points out that a spiritual path and a religious path are different: "Spirituality has nothing to do with religion. If spirituality is a living garden where beautiful flowers are growing, religion is a museum where all those once-beautiful flowers are now wilting...While religion emerges out of the mind of man mostly for his selfish desires, spirituality takes birth in the longing heart of an individual. Spirituality is an existential longing to know who you are; it is the desire of the universe to know itself through you."

Later discussions synthesize and further illustrate this concept: "Spirituality is always a leap of faith. It's like walking to the edge of the mountain and jumping off without worrying whether you are wearing a parachute, or if someone is down there to catch your fall. That moment of trust when you reach deep within and take the leap, is the moment of your spiritual liberation. The rest of the journey is simply to realize the fact that you have already found what you are looking for."

Readers unfamiliar with these processes may initially believe this discussion will revolve around philosophical or ethereal concepts of higher purpose, but there's a grounded benefit to many of these approaches that translates to improved everyday life. One example lies in pain sufferers: "When you watch the pain intensely, the energy of watching completely transforms the way you experience pain. Although the source of pain is in the body, it is the mind that makes it real. Mind controls everything, including the sensations of physical pain. When you gain control over your mind, you gain control over physical pain as well."

As Avi applies the concepts and approaches of spiritual enlightenment and meditation to every facet of daily living, readers come to understand that the benefits of following this silent path go beyond enlightenment on the spiritual realm to permeate every facet of life.

As an anecdote to the Culture of Doubt, The Silent Path: Awaken to Your Highest Possibility is more than just uplifting. It's simple, achievable, and easy for anybody to digest. It offers a course of action and a set of admonitions that should resonate with a wide audience, lies within no single religious realm, and can be understood and applied to all lives, across the board.

Those with an interest in self-help and spiritual growth will find The Silent Path an excellent beginning to embarking on a different life journey grounded in the pursuit of happiness and renewed purpose.

Diane Donovan, Senior Editor
Midwest Book Review

Introduction

In a world filled with noise and distractions, where the pace of life can be overwhelming, there lies a path rarely noticed—a path of profound silence, waiting patiently to be discovered. It is on this path that the true essence of existence reveals itself, where one can embark on a journey of self-discovery and transformation. Welcome to "The Silent Path - Awaken to your Highest Possibility."

Within the pages of this book, we embark on an exploration of the fundamental questions that have puzzled humanity since time immemorial. What is an individual? What lies at the core of our being? Can we truly understand the nature of the mind and its intricate workings? These questions have fascinated seekers and philosophers throughout history, and in our quest for meaning, we are drawn closer to understanding the depths of our existence.

We dive into the enigmatic relationship between the mind, body, and self, uncovering the interconnectedness that shapes our human experience. Through the lens of ancient wisdom and contemporary insights, we unravel the tapestry of consciousness, revealing the profound ways in which our thoughts, emotions, and perceptions shape our reality.

Meditation, a practice revered by sages and mystics for centuries, takes center stage in our exploration. We venture into the realm of stillness and presence, peeling back the layers of restlessness to embrace the power of silence. Through practical guidance and profound insights, we discover the transformative potential that lies within each breath and the limitless possibilities that await when we turn our attention inward.

But why embark on such a journey? What drives us to search for awakening? We seek answers beyond the confines of fleeting happiness and external achievements. We yearn for a deeper understanding of our purpose, our interconnectedness, and the ultimate truth that lies beyond the illusions of the world. The quest for awakening becomes an inherent part of our human nature - an invitation to step into the fullness of our being and unlock our highest potential.

In our exploration, we challenge the conventional notions of knowledge and information. We recognize that true wisdom resides not in the accumulation of facts, but in the profound integration of knowledge into lived experience. We navigate the vast ocean of information that inundates our modern lives, distilling the essence that leads us to true understanding and genuine transformation.

And finally, we venture into the realm of enlightenment - a state of being that transcends the limitations of the individual self and embraces the expansive nature of universal consciousness. Drawing inspiration from the enlightened beings who have graced our world, we unravel the mysteries of this profound awakening, and the profound liberation it brings.

"The Silent Path - Awaken to your Highest Possibility" is an invitation to embark on a journey of self-discovery, a roadmap for those seeking to transcend the limitations of ordinary existence and step into the boundless potential of their being. It is a guidebook, bridging ancient wisdom and modern insights, empowering readers to find solace in the silence, clarity in the chaos, and the courage to embrace their highest possibility. Let the whispers of the silent path guide you as you embark on this transformative odyssey of awakening.

THE INDIVIDUAL

"Be yourself; everyone else is already taken."

Oscar Wilde

What exactly does it mean to be an individual? Who is an individual?

The next time you step outside, take a look at all the life that surrounds you. Observe the insects buzzing around and the birds singing their songs, living their simple lives without any worries or troubles. They are just present in the moment, experiencing a state of peace and contentment that can be considered blissful.

When you look up to see a bird soaring in the sky, take a moment to appreciate its effortless grace and freedom. Unlike us humans, this bird has no religion, no name, and is unaware of its origins and destination. It doesn't have any philosophy or ideology and doesn't believe in concepts like heaven and hell or redemption. But despite all this, the bird still embodies a sense of peace and liberation as it glides through the endless sky. If we can strive to embody even just a moment of this same freedom, we will understand the true value and power of our individual selves.

We are like oceans, deep and complex in nature, with our true selves extending beyond our physical appearance. The image we see in the mirror is just a reflection, created by the play of light and shadow. Turn off the light, and the image disappears. But what remains unseen is the pulsating consciousness that animates our being, through which we are able to ponder, "This is my body."

The thought of "I Am" is what sets us apart from other beings and gives us a unique individual identity. Not all creatures with a physical form are considered individuals, as individuality arises from the contemplation of the concept of "I." The birth of individuality is not tied to the body, but rather to the inception of the "I Am" thought.

However, this self-awareness can also be a double-edged sword. If we had never realized our individuality, we would have lived a carefree life like animals, existing purely as a part of the natural world, without the need to question our purpose or envy the freedom of birds flying in the sky.

Now that we are aware of ourselves, we are on a constant quest to discover the truth about our identity and the purpose of our existence. Our lives are a journey to answer the fundamental question of "Who am I?" and the lack of understanding about our true selves is what causes our fears, frustrations, and sufferings.

Our modern world may be filled with technological advancements and convenience, but it hasn't brought us any closer to true happiness and fulfillment. In fact, it could be argued that we are struggling more than ever to find peace and purpose in life. Despite all the intelligence and sophistication we possess, our ignorance remains, perpetuated by the very things that we believe bring us comfort.

As individuals, we are often consumed by the expectations and norms of society, making it difficult to truly understand who we are and our place in the world. Unfortunately, most systems in place do not focus on individual liberation and self-discovery, but rather their own preservation and growth. It falls on each person to break free from these constraints and embark on their own journey of self-discovery.

The essence of individuality has been suffocated by our collective obsession with material success. Understanding what it means to be an individual is crucial, not only for the individual but for the future of humanity as a whole. This journey of self-inquiry is unique to each person, as their understanding of self is unique. Society may provide external frameworks, but it is up to the individual to delve within and find their own truth.

By asking the question "Who am I?" you set yourself on a path of self-discovery and personal growth. This journey may be challenging, but the reward is a greater sense of purpose, clarity, and meaning in life.

Spirituality is not confined to any set religion or belief system. It's a personal journey, a quest for self-discovery that transcends cultural and religious boundaries. It's about seeking the truth of our existence, finding inner peace, and meaning in life.

Religion, on the other hand, is a structured set of beliefs and practices that center around doctrines and ceremonies. While religion can offer comfort and community for some, it can also restrict an individual's ability to think critically and form their own opinions and understanding of life.

To grasp the true essence of individuality, we need to look inward and embark on a spiritual journey, rather than relying solely on the teachings of religion. This journey involves self-reflection, introspection, and an openness to the unknown. By delving into the depths of our consciousness, we can gain a deeper insight into our unique identity and place in the world.

In spirituality, you are in the driver's seat, you're the boss, and you're in control of your journey. You decide where you want to go and how you want to get there. It's a journey of self-exploration and self-awareness. On the flip side, in religion, you give up control, you follow the rules, you let others guide you, and you have no say in the direction of your journey. You depend on someone else's views, teachings, and guidance.

Both religion and spirituality can provide comfort and direction to individuals, but it's crucial to understand that they are different paths and one should choose what aligns with their innermost self. It's essential to find your own truth, delve into your own experiences, and form your own beliefs. The journey of self-discovery through spirituality is a journey towards becoming a complete, unified individual, not just a follower of a set of rigid rules.

Indeed, modern life has given us many luxuries and advancements that were once impossible, but it has also created a void in terms of spiritual connection and purpose. The fast-paced advancements of technology have left many of us feeling confused and disconnected, searching for a deeper meaning.

But, modernization has also given us an opportunity to explore spirituality on our own terms, without any limitations imposed by society or religion. Having the ability to choose is a powerful weapon, and we can use it to reconnect with our inner selves and find purpose in life.

At the end of the day, the journey towards self-discovery is a personal one, and it's up to each of us to choose the path we want to take and the meaning we want to find. Whether it's through spirituality, religion, or something else, the key is to never stop searching and to keep an open mind.

Nowadays, individuals are no longer restricted by religion, race, gender, or ethnicity. This presents a unique opportunity for individuals to rediscover their true selves and find meaning in life. With this newfound freedom, though, comes great responsibility. It's up to each person to use their newfound power wisely. More than ever before, the future of humanity lies in the hands of free-thinking individuals.

Being an individual means having the courage to question what society says, to look beyond the norms and beliefs that have been passed down to us, and to forge our own path. It requires us to be self-aware, to take responsibility for our thoughts, emotions, and actions, and to live a life that is true to ourselves and not just what others expect of us.

The concept of heresy has changed over time, and many societies now value individual freedom of thought and expression. But we still face remnants of oppressive systems and ideologies that try to limit our thinking and expression. It's our job to recognize these remnants and assert our right to think and express ourselves freely, to find our own truth.

We are shaped by our past, our upbringing, cultural background, and historical events, but it's important to question these influences and challenge our beliefs, especially if they stop us from thinking freely. This journey of self-discovery and self-realization is personal and requires introspection, a willingness to question our beliefs and experiences. And by doing so, we can truly start to understand who we are as individuals and have the power to shape our lives and the future of humanity.

It's high time for individuals to shed the shackles of their past, open their minds to new ideas, and strive towards a deeper understanding of themselves, paving the way for a brighter and more meaningful future.

WE ARE ASLEEP

"I love sleep. My life has a tendency to fall apart when I'm awake, you know?"

Ernest Hemingway

What is sleep?

As human beings, we have the choice to live our lives either lost in our thoughts or fully present in the moment. Unfortunately, the former is a more common state for many of us. Just take a walk in the city, or anywhere for that matter, and observe the people around you. You'll see that many of them are walking and talking without being fully mindful of their actions. This is just one example of how much of life can pass us by without our full awareness and attention.

It's almost as if we're sleepwalking through our waking hours, lost in our thoughts. Just like when we sleep, our physical bodies become unaware and we drift into our thoughts. During the day, we may become lost in thought and forget about our physical surroundings for a short period of time. This is like being in a state of sleep, where we're not fully aware of our physical bodies. But, we don't typically recognize this as sleep because it can be unsettling to think of ourselves as sleepwalking through the day. The only time we're truly awake and present is when we're fully conscious and aware of our physical surroundings in the present moment.

Many individuals live their lives in a state of mental distraction or unconsciousness, much like sleep-walking. In this state, our ideas and concepts about reality remain just that - ideas. We may talk about spirituality, the afterlife, consciousness, or energy, but as long as we're lost in thought, these remain merely abstract concepts. Our thoughts and thinking become all-consuming, preventing us from fully experiencing life and the world around us. However, true wakefulness and presence allow us to move beyond abstract concepts and ideas and engage with the world on a deeper level.

There's a level of consciousness beyond the norms of sleeping and being awake, called enlightenment or awakening. It's a state that can be achieved through deep meditation and is characterized by a loss of physical body awareness and the stopping of thoughts, emotions, and desires. This state allows one to experience pure existence and the true essence of their self, free from limiting beliefs or preconceptions. It's a state that cannot be fully expressed through words, but must be experienced directly.

In the state of awakening, there's a feeling of pure liveliness that surpasses all limits and boundaries. It lies beyond the confines of time and space, and isn't restricted by any beliefs or concepts. This is the core of one's true self and the ultimate state of being. By practicing deep meditation and reaching a state of "Samadhi" or "Equal-Mindedness," individuals can experience a limitless sense of aliveness and transcend the boundaries of daily life. Surprisingly, everyone already exists in this state of pure being, but are unaware of it.

We are all living in a sea of existence, but often remain unaware of its vastness. Our daily activities such as dreaming, walking, creating, and even life and death are all sustained by this aliveness. Yet, this aliveness remains hidden from us as we get lost in our thoughts, consumed by our dreams. Like a fish in the ocean, we are surrounded by life, yet remain unaware of its true essence.

There is a fundamental difference between living with the belief that our lives are confined to our mortal bodies and recognizing that our minds and bodies are simply expressions of our infinite and eternal Self. This distinction separates the enlightened from the rest of us. While an enlightened person may also be physically bound by their body, they understand that a part of them extends beyond the limits of the body, bringing them freedom and happiness. Conversely, the rest of us live and die as part of life's dream, trapped by the illusion of a transitory mind and body. In this dream, we experience birth and death, never truly realizing our true nature.

The ultimate spiritual objective for individuals should be to reach a state of transcendence that goes beyond the limitations of mind and body. This journey of self-discovery may take time and effort, but with dedication and consistent practice, you can eventually learn to release your attachment to your physical body, although this doesn't mean you can physically separate from your body and levitate.

True detachment is a mental state, even though your physical body remains bound. When you are detached from body consciousness, you can feel a sense of freedom and liberation, despite being physically limited. This seemingly paradoxical state is achievable with hard work and practice.

Why is this state of detachment so crucial? It's essential because true happiness and contentment cannot be attained when you are in bondage. The human mind is plagued by a unique form of pain, leading to chaos, confusion, and suffering. This pain is not experienced by animals because they lack self-awareness, and it's not experienced by enlightened individuals because they are fully self-aware. Awakened individuals may experience physical pain, emotional pain, or the pain of loss or rejection, but there is another type of pain deeply ingrained in the human psyche that they do not experience, and that is the pain of not knowing one's true self.

We often go about our lives lost in thought, ignoring the reality that we are living in a dream-like state. The dream is not just something we experience at night, but it encompasses every aspect of our existence. From the people we interact with, to the places we visit, to the things we do, it all exists in this dream. And, we have become so deeply invested in this dream that we have accepted it as our one and only reality.

Despite our bodies constantly reminding us that we cannot stay here forever, we still avoid facing the fundamental questions of our existence. To escape these questions, we keep ourselves busy, constantly engaging in activities like socializing, traveling, or planning for the future. This is why finding stillness and quiet is such a difficult task. Our minds have become too accustomed to being distracted, making it easier to watch a movie or hang out with friends than to sit in quiet meditation.

The struggle to find stillness and quiet reveals a deeper issue within us. It suggests that there is a lot of pain and fear within us that we want to avoid. We distract ourselves with external activities because we fear the unknown aspects of ourselves. The fear of uncovering these unknown parts of us creates a reluctance to be alone with our thoughts, almost as if we are afraid of ourselves. This is why the simple act of sitting quietly can be such a daunting challenge for many people.

Every day, the sun rises and puts on a show for us, reminding us that it is not as rigid as it seems. It moves from east to west, playing with our emotions and moods in a mysterious way. Yet, we look at this incredible aspect of life and brush it off, saying, "Oh, there's nothing mysterious about the sun. We all know what it is. It's just a ball of gas that produces heat and light through nuclear fusion." While this explanation may be true in a technical sense, what is the sun really? No one truly knows, and that is its enigmatic quality.

The clouds float in the sky, changing shape, size, color, and beauty, reminding us of the dreamlike, mystical nature of existence. We explain to our children that clouds are formed from water vapor that rises into the sky and eventually falls as rain. While this may be true logically, why should this logical understanding stop us from pausing and appreciating the clouds for their mysterious beauty? It's much better to embrace the ever-changing nature of existence and go with the flow, rather than trying to impose our fixed ideas on it.

Understanding the balance between logic and mysticism is not always easy, but sometimes embracing the latter can bring a deeper appreciation for life. Imagine viewing existence as a constantly evolving canvas, with the clouds as masterful paintings that change form and color, reflecting the moods of the sky. This interpretation brings a level of personal connection to everything in existence, as it's all linked to your emotions, thoughts, and desires.

The reality of life is subjective, shaped by your perspective and how you choose to see it. Ponder these questions: Who experiences the colors of the sky? What is the purpose of everything in the world without your consciousness, dreams, and aspirations? And can anything truly exist independently of your perception?

The truth is, no matter where you are, life is always flowing around you and has a personal connection to you and your desires. Embracing this mystical view of existence can bring a deeper sense of wonder and magic to your life.

If you look at the world with a fresh pair of eyes, free from any preconceived notions or biases, you'll see just how ephemeral and dream-like reality is. Reality is like a ripple in water, constantly changing and evolving. This constant change in everything should make it clear that we don't live in a fixed or absolute reality. If that were the case, there would be moments when everything stays the same. But if you pay close attention, you'll see that everything is always in motion and that no two moments in life are ever the same.

Try this experiment: Grab your camera and head outside. Try to take two photos of the same thing, just two seconds apart. If you succeed, then you've found reality. But when you look at the photos, you'll see that they're different. Maybe the clouds have shifted, some leaves have moved, a different bird is perched on a branch, or something else has changed. This proves that no two photos and no two moments in life are identical.

In reality, there is nothing that is constant or fixed. Everything is always changing and evolving, and we're just a part of this process. To truly understand life, we need to step back from all our accumulated beliefs and ideas. We need to experience reality as it is, without any preconceived notions. Conceptually, the sun is a celestial body at the center of the solar system that keeps planets in orbit and generates light and heat that sustains life. But when we see it from a personal perspective, the sun can be seen as something completely different, with its own unique qualities.

Let's say you go without sunlight for a week, and then suddenly the first rays of the sun reach your skin. When you feel the warmth penetrate your body and touch your soul, you will understand what the sun truly is. It is not just an idea or concept, but a manifestation of life itself. In that moment, when the warm rays reach you, you will realize that there is a part of you in the sun and a part of the sun in you. This personal connection cannot be described with words or concepts. What you have experienced is a deeper unity of life, of which you are an integral part.

What is water? Can it be defined simply as a chemical compound composed of hydrogen and oxygen atoms? Or as a clear, flavorless, and odorless liquid? The most meaningful definition of water is that it satisfies thirst. Any other definitions or explanations of water only tell half the story. The other half lies within you, in your desire for water. Without considering your thirst and need for water, all definitions of water are incomplete. This applies to everything in existence. Describing life without considering the individual's experiences and perspectives is like a journey without the traveler - It lacks meaning.

Nature represents the unconscious part of your dreaming process and reflects the sum total of your fears and desires developed in your early childhood years. This is why you feel a powerful attraction to it. Nature is a perfect balance of beauty and cruelty, and it is impossible to understand its purpose without understanding your role in its creation.

If nature is considered the foundation of life, how can it be seen as distinct from the one perceiving it? Can anything truly exist without someone to observe it? What color is a rainbow when there's no one there to see it? Nature is a reflection of our thoughts, dreams, and desires, and if we have trouble grasping this concept, it's likely because of our tendency to view life objectively and scientifically, rather than through personal experiences and emotions. For an idea to be considered true, it must not only make logical sense but also resonate emotionally with the observer.

In our quest for objective science, we've separated ourselves from nature and reality. We've come up with numerous theories and ideas about life, but in doing so, we've lost touch with the true essence of life. Our story only makes sense when it's viewed within the context of the earth, sky, animals, stars, and everything else that exists.

Each individual's story is intertwined with the story of nature, and we can't fully understand ourselves without understanding our connection to the natural world. The closer we are to nature, the clearer our understanding of life becomes. Without this connection, our sense of purpose and meaning is diminished. While we can survive in artificial environments, true living requires a deep connection to the natural world.

To truly understand life, we must look at it holistically. Analyzing a flower by dissecting it won't give us a complete understanding of its essence. A flower only makes sense in its connection to the plant. To truly comprehend the flower, we must consider its relationship with the plant. This detached and disconnected way of examining life and our place in the universe is a major flaw in our approach to uncovering our true identity.

Analysis provides limited information about something that's already known. Analyzing the chemical composition of salt won't answer philosophical questions like why salt is salty or why there is such a thing as salt. These fundamental questions about life can't be answered through analysis alone. To truly understand, we must look at life as a whole, not just its individual parts. The reality that surrounds us provides important clues to our internal reality, and our dreams and fascinations offer insight into our search for truth.

It's easy to get lost in thoughts, whether they're our own or someone else's. Everything we see around us, from the walls, windows, and chairs to the tables and other objects, was once just an idea in someone's mind. Physicality is just a manifestation of thought. It takes time and effort to turn an idea into a physical object, which we perceive as physicality. When we imagine a chair, there's no effort involved, so we simply call it a thought. But when we invest time and effort to turn that idea into a tangible object, it becomes real. This process applies to everything that's ever been created. So what distinguishes a dream from reality? The difference is minimal. Reality is just a tangible dream. Thoughts are the foundation of life, and turning those thoughts into reality is dreaming. Physicality can't exist without a thought, and thoughts and dreaming can't exist without sleep.

WHO IS SUFFERING?

"I have a great deal of suffering in my life. Most of which has never happened."

Mark Twain

Many spiritual teachers have said that the source of suffering is within, as in "we are the root cause of our suffering". How do we use this to understand the suffering we see in the world? For example, how can an individual who is suffering from slavery be responsible for it? I just feel that there is a contradiction here.

When a spiritual teacher tells you that the root of pain lies within you, they're not just talking about your mind and body. They're pointing to a deeper, more universal aspect of yourself that goes beyond physical and mental experiences.

When you grasp your true identity, the core of who you are, and the truth of your existence, you'll understand that nothing can happen without first going through your consciousness, even if you're not always aware of it. This is why a teacher often refers to the Self as being all-encompassing and all-knowing. Someone who has attained this understanding sees that there are no accidents in life. Pain is not a deliberate act, but an experience. It has no significance unless the Self is involved. In other words, pain can't exist without the participation of the Self.

If you delve deeply into the reasons for pain, whether it's your own or someone else's, you'll find that the source of suffering always comes from within. For example, when we see someone in pain, we also feel pain. If we're not suffering with that person, then we can't truly understand their pain. Every time we witness someone in agony, something within us also hurts. The source of suffering isn't in the person, but within us. When we recognize the suffering of others or the suffering in the world, we do so through our own experiences. It's impossible to grasp suffering without experiencing it ourselves. If we're content, we can't talk about or contemplate suffering objectively.

The teacher knows that our struggles are all connected, and there's a deeper meaning behind the events and situations we face. When we look at things through the narrow lens of our minds and bodies, it may seem like we're not in control of our suffering and that it's just happening to us. But it's all a matter of perception. From the perspective of our minds, suffering may seem to come from outside, but when seen through the eyes of the Self, we realize how we've contributed to our own pain.

If we see ourselves only as the body, we'll never fully escape suffering. Our bodies will always experience some form of pain. But when we let go of the body consciousness and drift off to sleep, the suffering disappears. For instance, if someone cuts their finger and feels pain, that pain disappears when they fall asleep. This shows that suffering is directly tied to our attachment to the physical form. The less we cling to our bodies, the less suffering we'll endure.

It's amazing to think that we have the potential to experience life beyond just the physical realm, but it all starts with a shift in our beliefs. Society has conditioned us to see everything in terms of physical cause and effect, but if we want to transcend suffering, we need to challenge that notion. We have to have faith in our own existence beyond just our physical form. This is the heart of spirituality, and it's what sets us apart from other species.

We live in a mysterious, spiritual world, but we tend to cling to materialistic ideas. Our education, upbringing, and social interactions have mostly focused on physical reality, leading us to believe that we are just our bodies. Our minds try to explain everything through that lens, but we don't question whether consciousness can truly emerge from physical processes. Despite its limitations, this materialistic view of life is appealing, and we often adopt it without fully considering its implications.

We consider an idea or theory to be true when it gains widespread support, and that's what's happened with our understanding of consciousness. Instead of exploring it for ourselves, we've accepted the theory that it arises from our brains. But have we asked ourselves, "Is my body producing my consciousness, or is my consciousness producing my body?" When we meditate, there's a moment when the body seems to shut off, but we remain aware. This is when we realize that the body is a manifestation of consciousness, not the other way around. In that moment, we understand that we are something much more subtle and mysterious, beyond just our physical form.

As we consider the questions of how to handle the suffering in our lives and in the world, it's crucial to take into account the era we're living in. Many spiritual teachings from the past may not hold the same relevance today.

For instance, if you were born 300 years ago, your community would have been much smaller, and you would have only witnessed suffering firsthand. But with the rise of technology, we're now exposed to suffering not only in the moment, but repeated and amplified through media. This constant exposure to violence and pain has added a new dimension to our suffering, moving it from physical to mental.

Think about it, if someone fell from a tree and broke their back 100 years ago in a small village, the suffering would have only impacted the immediate community. People would have felt the pain and offered help. However, today, if someone has a similar accident, the video could easily be posted online or on TV, where hundreds or thousands of people could watch it repeatedly, causing widespread suffering from a single event. Technology has made it easier for suffering to spread beyond its original location.

In today's world, it can be easy to become overwhelmed by the constant exposure to suffering through digital media. It can make us feel guilty for not doing enough to help, and the task of alleviating the suffering of the entire world can seem impossible. The world is more complex now than it used to be, and trying to solve all of its problems can lead to feelings of helplessness.

In the past, when the world was limited to what one could see on foot, making a difference, spreading love and compassion, could be done within one's own community. But without understanding the realities of today's world, a loving and compassionate nature can actually lead to further suffering. The best way to approach this issue is to understand it from a personal perspective. Knowing our own limitations and what we can and cannot do can make a huge difference. When we realize that the root cause of suffering lies within us, we can take steps to overcome it.

In her grief, Kisa Gotami went to Buddha and asked, "What prayers, what magical incantations do you have to bring my son back to life?"

Instead of sending her away or reasoning with her, Buddha said to her, "Fetch me a mustard seed from a home that has never known sorrow. We will use it to drive the sorrow out of your life." The woman went off at once in search of that magical mustard seed.

She came first to a splendid mansion, knocked at the door, and said, "I am looking for a home that has never known sorrow. Is this such a place? It is very important to me."

They told her, "You've certainly come to the wrong place," and began to describe all the tragic things that recently had befallen them.

The woman said to herself, "Who is better able to help these poor, unfortunate people than I, who have had the misfortune of my own?" She stayed to comfort them, then went on in search of a home that had never known sorrow. But wherever she turned, she found one tale after another of sadness and misfortune.

The woman became so involved in helping others cope with their sorrows that she eventually let go of her own. She would later come to understand that it was the quest to find the magical mustard seed that drove away her suffering.

The reason why Buddha was seen as selfish by some people is because he chose to focus on his own inner journey of self-discovery, rather than trying to alleviate suffering in his immediate surroundings. His wife, for instance, thought he was harsh and insensitive for leaving her and their child without a word. However, Buddha understood that the source of suffering lies within each individual, and that the only way to truly overcome it was to look inward. This takes a keen intellect and the courage to go against societal norms, as it's much easier to just go along with the crowd and share in their suffering.

True compassion is not just about crying with those who are in pain, but rather, it's about finding joy and hope even amidst adversity. This is what enlightened teachers like Buddha taught their followers - a way to transcend suffering and find true happiness. Rather than just offering a temporary fix, they showed people how to overcome their own suffering and find peace. This is what makes them true contributors to the world and to humanity.

People may see enlightened teachers as cold and indifferent because they don't put a lot of stock in addressing someone's emotional wants. This is because doing so just keeps the suffering going, it doesn't end it. Unfortunately, some people find comfort in suffering and even crave it, as it can bring attention and validation from others.

When life is good, we tend to go through it alone, but when we're facing challenges, we often look for support and comfort from others, just like a child running to their mom after getting hurt. This kind of behavior can continue into adulthood, leading to an attachment to suffering. To grow spiritually, we have to move past this immature clinging to suffering and learn to handle difficulties on our own.

Empathizing with those who are suffering just perpetuates their suffering. This isn't true compassion. Instead, it reinforces it. When we understand that a person's suffering is driven by emotional needs, it's important to be careful not to fuel those needs and create an unhealthy dependence. Caring for someone is different. If a person's physical body is in pain, we can care for it. And in some cases, individuals may not be able to care for themselves and may need our support. But it's important to avoid supporting imaginary or emotional suffering, and instead, find its root cause. The source of all suffering lies within us, and the key to transcending it is to distance ourselves from it, not engage with it.

In order to help someone overcome their suffering, we must equip them with the tools to do so. This is where spirituality and meditation come in - they offer methods to go beyond suffering. Even small steps like meditating for an hour each day can make a big difference in transcending suffering. By taking the time to reflect and identify the root cause of their pain, individuals can start the journey towards freedom from it.

Everyone's suffering is unique to them. Although we may all experience suffering at some point, the specifics of a person's pain are entirely their own. No one can alleviate another person's suffering. So, it's crucial for individuals to learn how to cope with their own pain so they can then offer support to others. Just like two people drowning in water, if neither knows how to swim, they can't save each other. One must have the knowledge and skills to help the other. To be truly compassionate and empathetic, we must first master our own suffering and then extend that understanding to others.

Suffering should be a rare, minor occurrence in our lives. However, because people try to help others without knowing how to distance themselves from suffering, they often become consumed by it themselves when trying to assist others. Think about it - our own suffering may not have been intense, but it can feel like a never-ending experience when we constantly witness the pain of those around us.

If you want to avoid suffering, it's simple: pick the place where there's peace instead of where people are talking about suffering. Whether it's a physical place or a thought in your mind, distance yourself from sources of suffering to find peace. If you find that your mind is constantly dwelling on negative things, it's time to take control. This is where meditation comes in - it helps us observe our thoughts and choose not to engage with the ones that cause discomfort. By mastering our thoughts, we can go beyond suffering and find inner peace. Once we've found enlightenment, we can spread positivity and compassion simply by being present. The key to compassion is to make sure that no one can cause us more suffering than what we can handle through our own conscious decisions.

YOU ARE NOT YOUR THOUGHTS

"Don't believe everything you think. Thoughts are just that - thoughts."

Allan Lokos

Today in my meditation I was stuck because I realized that I didn't have any idea what a thought was. I was thinking and thinking about trying to stop thinking. All the while, I didn't even know what a thought was. What exactly is a thought?

You could have just as easily asked, "What is life?" or "What is the universe?" Thoughts are not isolated entities or physical objects that can be seen and touched. To truly understand what a thought is, we need to look at the perspective of the person asking the question. For the person asking, thoughts are a mystery, and they want to comprehend their nature and purpose. So, who is this questioner and why do they want to know about thoughts?

But when you take a closer look, you may realize that you are not the only one asking this question. The question arises from a thought itself, as if the thought is trying to understand itself. The inquiry into "What is a thought?" is itself a thought, so it cannot be considered solely your question. Although you're asking it, the question is being channeled through you. It's not necessarily your personal desire to understand thoughts, but rather the desire of the thought process itself. This is how deeply our thoughts can control and consume us.

Distinguishing ourselves from our thoughts can be a challenging task. We're so intertwined with our thoughts that it can be difficult to define a thought directly. The only way to truly grasp the nature of a thought is by transcending thoughts entirely. When we reach a state of mind where thoughts are absent and there is complete stillness, that's when we can comprehend what a thought truly is.

Imagine a light has been on for an indefinite amount of time. It can be tough to explain what light is without turning it off. The best we can do is describe it as a force that allows us to see things. Light can't be physically pointed to and identified as a separate entity, but we can understand it through its effects, like illuminating objects and making them visible. If someone has a hard time believing in or comprehending light, the easiest solution is to turn off the light and observe the change in visibility. In that moment, they'll understand the function of light, even if they don't know its exact composition or nature. Similarly, taking a moment to quiet our thoughts can give us insight into the purpose and meaning of thoughts and why we're constantly thinking.

The reason why our minds generate thoughts is still not fully understood. At the moment, we're constantly surrounded by thoughts. There's rarely a moment when our minds aren't in thought. The abundance of thoughts makes it hard to understand the nature of a thought, not because of a lack of knowledge, but because of the overwhelming presence of thoughts. Every image we see in our mind is a thought, every scent we detect is a thought, every sensation we feel is a thought, and even our physical bodies are forms of thought.

Thoughts aren't just mental images that pop in and out of our minds. They're deeply ingrained in the way our minds work and extend beyond that. Thoughts shape our bodies, actions, and desires, influencing everything in our lives. The goal of meditation is to reach a state of thoughtlessness, where the mind is free and empty. This can bring about a powerful realization: even without thoughts, the self still exists. Despite not thinking about the body, mind, or world, the self remains present and unchanged.

When the Buddha was asked what the ultimate experience of enlightenment was like, he referred to it as "Nothingness". The beauty of this word is that, even though it represents a moment without thoughts, there is still someone experiencing "Nothingness". It is the individual who is experiencing this state, even though there are no physical or tangible objects involved. The absence of thought doesn't mean there is a lack of existence or experience. In this state of "Nothingness" or Nirvana, the person still exists, just without the influence or presence of thoughts.

This can be hard to grasp if we only look at things from a materialistic standpoint. If we believe that we are limited to just our physical bodies and nothing more, it becomes challenging to understand what thoughts really are. From a materialistic point of view, thoughts can be seen as nothing more than electrical signals in the brain, produced by neurons. According to this viewpoint, all experiences in life are stored in the mind as thoughts, and when we want to recall something, we rekindle that thought and relive the memory. While this explanation might seem simple, it's limited and not entirely accurate.

Thoughts are not just limited to electrical or chemical processes in the brain. Instead, they are a universal phenomenon that encompasses everything in existence. The universe, our minds, and our bodies are all made up of thoughts. There is nothing in the universe that isn't part of the thought process. That's why Buddha said that you are nothing but your thoughts. He understood the all-encompassing nature of thoughts and their powerful influence on everything.

If you have a materialistic perspective, it's easy to misinterpret the saying "You are nothing but your thoughts" to mean "I can't exist without my thoughts." This can lead to the belief that you need to constantly be thinking in order to exist. However, that's not accurate. In fact, the mere act of looking at yourself in a mirror is a result of a thought. Our self-image is created by thoughts, and without them, we wouldn't even be able to see or feel our own body. So, it's important to ask yourself, "Who's asking the question about thoughts? Is it me or is it a thought asking?"

Asking questions about thoughts will only lead to more questions if the inquiry is just a byproduct of the thought process. The more you try to understand thoughts, the more thoughts you'll generate, leaving you with a bunch of ideas without any real clarity. Simply ruminating on thoughts won't give you a deeper understanding of them. The only way to comprehend thoughts is to experience a state of no thought.

Just like a person who has lived in the ocean their whole life may not fully grasp the concept of water despite many explanations, they can only truly understand water by stepping out of the ocean for a moment and then returning to it. While swimming in the ocean, our awareness of it was limited because we weren't focused on it. Whether we knew what the ocean was or not, we could still survive, just like a fish can live without knowing anything about water.

We are part of the infinite sea of life and awareness, just like fish in the ocean, not realizing the essence that sustains us. But, unlike fish, we have the ability to question: "What is a thought? What is the mind? What is the body? What is the true nature of reality around us?" This is where the journey of exploration and discovery begins. By asking these questions, we delve deeper into the fabric of existence, seeking to understand what everything, including ourselves, is made of. When we truly comprehend what thoughts are, we will also understand our true self.

Thoughts are like clouds in the sky of consciousness, which represents our true being. The vastness of the sky represents what we seek. Currently, the sky is obscured by our thoughts, and we have each identified with a single cloud, made up of our name, form, actions, and desires, all accumulated over time.

Our lives started with a single desire, and from there, we collected more and more clouds of thoughts. Now, our sky is obscured by a thick layer of thinking, and every question we ask is about the cloud. We ask about its shape, color, and contents, rather than the sky itself. When we inquire about enlightenment, we ask when the cloud will dissipate, so we can see the sky. But, it is still the cloud that is asking the question. Our clouds are made of thoughts and nothing more, layer upon layer of never-ending thoughts. The real us is hidden behind the cloud, waiting to be uncovered.

In order to gain a better understanding of thoughts, it's important to acknowledge that we're not one with our thoughts. We can generate thoughts, toy with them, engage with them, and then let them go, moving on to new ones. Throughout our lives, we've been interacting with thoughts, but we've never become those thoughts. Our sense of self remains constant, right? When you were five years old, you had the same sense of self that you have now. Even when you wake up from sleep, you never feel confused about who you are, despite being unconscious for several hours.

If we were just thoughts, this unchanging sense of self wouldn't be possible. We may get confused about various other things, but we never confuse ourselves with someone else. This means that there's something about us that remains separate from our thoughts - that doesn't get lost or mixed up with them. The question "What is a thought?" is profound because the answer to the ultimate question "What am I?" lies just beyond the veil of thoughts. Allow this question to torment you until the truth reveals itself.

The Silent Path

THE CREATIVE SELF

"I never made one of my discoveries through the process of rational thinking."

Albert Einstein

What is the connection between creativity and the individual?

Creativity is not just something that can be added to life as an extra; it is the very essence of life itself. Living is a creative act, and without you, creativity would not exist. Your mind has the power to imagine, form thoughts, and evoke emotions, and when you unleash these innate qualities, they turn into creativity. Everyone has the potential to be creative, it's not something you can opt out of. Saying, "I don't want to be creative, I'll just stick to my normal routine," just won't cut it.

When we fully engage in life, creativity is an inevitable outcome. Why would we ever want to ignore it? Our purpose is to express ourselves, and through this expression, our lives can attain meaning and significance. If we choose to suppress this, a part of us will remain unsatisfied, and we'll constantly feel incomplete. We must embrace creativity as an integral part of life. Without it, life becomes dull and uninspiring.

Creativity is a crucial component of human progress, and without it, we would never have seen the groundbreaking discoveries of scientists like Albert Einstein. Einstein himself attributed his scientific success to his imaginative abilities, which allowed him to perceive the world in new and unique ways. Though Einstein is remembered as a great scientist, he was also a visionary who saw the power of imagination over mere knowledge. He once said, "Imagination is more important than knowledge. Knowledge is limited to what we have learned, while imagination encompasses the entire world and all that will ever be known."

It's important to understand the difference between imagination and thinking. While thinking is simply recalling information that has already been learned, imagination is exploring uncharted territories of the mind. Einstein's imagination set him apart from his peers, as he placed a higher value on imagination over simple thinking.

The key to unlocking our imagination lies in the quiet and stillness of our minds. The chaos and noise of life can hinder imagination, which requires peace and calm to flourish. That's why meditation is so powerful for creativity - it helps us tap into our inner silence and stillness, just like preparing soil is crucial for gardening. By clearing out unwanted thoughts, we create space for imagination to grow and take root. Without inner peace and stillness, there will be no room for creativity to develop and thrive.

Imagine being consumed by anger and feeling agitated inside. In such a state, it would be impossible to be creative and solve any problems. Your mind, body, and energy would be completely absorbed by the anger, leaving no room for creative expression. This highlights the importance of inner peace as a prerequisite for creativity.

Many artists face the challenge of coming up with new ideas, no matter what their field of art may be. Whether they are painters, dancers, singers, or musicians, they all struggle with letting go of the past. For example, a composer can easily create a new melody if they can break free from the old tune that's stuck in their mind. To do this, they need to stop hearing their previous compositions, especially the successful ones, and enter a state of inner silence. This is where meditation comes in. By practicing meditation, we can reach a zone of peace and stillness within ourselves. Once we are in this calm space, creativity flows effortlessly.

I once had the chance to ask an Indian dancer about her creative process. Indian classical dance is a challenging art form that focuses more on the internal movement of emotions than on the external movements of the body. The goal of this ancient art is to tap into one's innermost depths and bring out their best qualities. Indian classical dance is a great way to express individuality. In order to seamlessly blend emotions and movements, the dancer must master the art of being fully present in the moment. Although the movements may be choreographed, the dancer still needs to improvise and add their personal touch and emotional awareness. This results in a unique expression for each dancer, reflected in their movements, interaction with the audience, and overall performance.

This dancer was an expert, with nearly three decades of experience in her art. She was renowned for her talent and was often sought after for her performances. When I asked her about her dancing, she told me about a realization she had after many years of performing. At first, she felt self-conscious on stage and struggled to incorporate improvisations into her dancing. But eventually, she realized that she was not actually the one dancing. Something beyond her took over during her performances and she was in a state of inner peace and stillness. She felt like someone else was performing the best parts of her dance. She was so in the zone that she was unaware of her movements, the audience, and the dance itself. After the performance, she'd come back to reality with the sound of applause.

Creativity is not something we actively produce, it arises from within us. It's a fundamental force that exists throughout existence, and the key to accessing it is to cultivate emptiness and let it unfold. Trying too hard to force creativity will only make it harder to come by. It cannot flourish under pressure, whether it's external or internal. By embracing stillness and living in the present moment, we can open ourselves up to the natural flow of creativity.

When the dancer was in a state of emptiness and stillness, pure creative energy flowed through her, transporting her to a transcendental realm. This is why she was unaware of the most intense moments of her dance. Many artists find that the more they focus on themselves as artists, the harder it is to create. This strong self-identification can lead to fears of rejection, difficulty in expressing oneself, and feelings of inadequacy. But by finding a place of inner peace and stillness, we can move beyond this self-identification and become channels for transcendental, extraordinary creative expression.

KNOWLEDGE VS INFORMATION

"The only true wisdom is in knowing you know nothing."

Socrates

I love learning and picking up information. It's something I really enjoy, and I feel like it makes me a better person. But, it seems like there is a haze of knowledge that is barricading me from life, not allowing me to experience life. How much knowledge is necessary on this path of self-discovery? How much of what I'm holding on to should I drop?

Knowledge is not just about knowing facts or data, but it's about having a deep understanding of a subject through our own experiences. This type of knowledge is invaluable, as it can't be taken away from us and it stays with us forever. On the other hand, information is temporary, and when we no longer need it, it's gone.

So, if you want to have true knowledge and not just information, it's essential to embrace experiences and challenge yourself to step out of your comfort zone. By doing so, you can gain a deeper understanding of the world and yourself, and this newfound knowledge will bring lightness and joy into your life. Embrace the power of knowledge through personal experience, and you'll find that life becomes much more fulfilling and meaningful.

Knowledge is something that is experienced and deeply understood through personal reflection and contemplation. It's not just something that we memorize and recall on demand. It's a deeper understanding of the world and our place in it, something that we carry with us and that shapes our worldview.

So, how much knowledge should we seek? The answer is simple: only as much as is necessary to lead a fulfilling life. We don't need to know everything in order to experience the richness and beauty of life. In fact, trying to acquire too much knowledge can be overwhelming and detract from our enjoyment of life. Instead, we should focus on gaining a deeper understanding of the things that truly matter to us, and let go of the rest. That way, we can live a life of purpose and clarity, without being bogged down by excess information.

As human beings, we accumulate both knowledge and information throughout our lives, but it's crucial to understand the difference between the two. Knowledge is the wisdom we gain from our personal experiences, shaping who we are and how we react to different situations. It's a part of us, not just something we recall. On the other hand, information is just data that we gather and recall when necessary, but it shouldn't define our identity or self-image.

We tend to hold onto information, giving it so much importance that we base our self-image on it. But, this self-image should be rooted in reality, not built upon mountains of information. Clinging to our self-image and knowledge can lead to unhappiness, as it's often not rooted in reality but in unrealistic ideals. The key to happiness is to let go of our self-image and embrace the present moment.

Knowledge is a source of wisdom and understanding, while information is just a tool that we use when necessary. It's important to seek knowledge and not just information, as knowledge should never weigh us down or cloud our perception of life, but rather embody the true essence of experiential wisdom.

In simpler terms, it's all about perspective. When we see information as just a tool that can be used when necessary and don't let it define who we are, then there's no harm in acquiring more of it. However, it's crucial to shed this information at the end of each day and return to our true self, living in the present moment and embracing each experience as new. That's when life becomes truly liberating.

The transformation from information to knowledge is an important step in our growth and understanding. Everything starts as information and it's up to us to turn it into knowledge through our experiences and personal integration. Gathering information is not a negative thing, but it's important to take the necessary steps to turn that information into knowledge for it to have a transformative effect on our lives.

In other words, information is just a stepping stone on the path to true knowledge. It's a tool that we use to get to where we want to be, but it's not the destination itself. Holding onto information once it's served its purpose is like continuing to carry the ladder after you've reached the top of the climb. The goal is to obtain a deep, personal understanding through experience, not to cling to the information used to get there.

This same concept applies to spirituality as well. As we journey towards a deeper understanding of ourselves, we come across various ideas and concepts that help us along the way. But it's important to remember that these ideas are just temporary tools, not absolute Truths to be imposed on others. When we forget this and start treating spiritual practices as rigid religious dogmas, we lose sight of the true purpose of our journey. The goal is to reach a place of authenticity and inner peace, not to be burdened by dogmatic beliefs.

It's important to understand the difference between spirituality and practicality. Just because we have learned spiritual teachings and ideas, it doesn't mean that they always have a practical application in our daily lives. When we try to impose these teachings as a way of life without fully understanding them, they can become limiting and dogmatic. The concepts and ideas introduced in spirituality are not absolute truths, but tools for personal growth and transformation.

As we continue on our spiritual journey, it's important to shed the information we have gathered and focus on the essence of spirituality, which is to discover our true selves and move beyond borrowed knowledge. Spirituality is not about collecting complex concepts and ideas, but rather about acquiring tools for self-discovery and growth.

While information can be easily quantified, true knowledge is immeasurable. We can only recognize our knowledge through the quality of our lives, such as our happiness, bliss, and contentment. If we are filled with only information, we often experience fear, stress, and unease. It's easy to tell the difference between someone who has gained experiential knowledge and someone who has only accumulated information by observing their level of joy. Ultimately, the most important thing to understand about knowledge and information is that while knowledge nourishes our soul, information only feeds our ego. Recognizing the difference between the two is true wisdom.

TRUST YOUR BODY

"If one observes, one will see that the body has its own intelligence; it requires a great deal of intelligence to observe the intelligence of the body."

Jiddu Krishnamurti

When I am observing the breath, I sometimes feel sensations in my forehead. Are these real? How do I know which body sensations are imagined and which are real?

As meditators, we must be aware of the difference between the experiences of our mind and body. These are two distinct experiences that should not be confused or merged. Understanding the distinction between these experiences is crucial in our journey to fully comprehend reality. Our minds tend to be consumed by thoughts and emotions, making it difficult to acknowledge other forms of experience beyond what is generated by our thoughts.

Let me give you an example. When I touch this cup of tea and feel its warmth, I'm having a bodily experience. Similarly, the sensation of weight in my hand and fingers is also a bodily experience. But as soon as I start thinking about the tea, like "I enjoy drinking tea," "This tea needs a little more sugar," or "This cup of tea is better than yesterday's," I've moved into a mental experience. That's the moment I shift from experiencing the tea with my body to evaluating it with my mind.

Did you catch how quickly this shift happened? As soon as I said "I enjoy drinking tea," I moved away from the bodily experience and into my mind. This is the process of getting lost in thoughts or daydreaming. Our mind is constantly evaluating the experiences of the body and becomes so absorbed in this process that it wanders off into thoughts. When we try to focus on our breath, for instance, the mind in the background is constantly trying to assess our actions. Before we know it, we're lost in thoughts about music or something else entirely. This is why it's important to stay present and not let our mind drift away from the experience at hand.

If you want to be present in the moment, it's important to understand the difference between the experiences of your body and the experiences of your mind. Pay attention to the real experiences happening in your body and be mindful of the imagined experiences happening in your mind. That's what meditation is all about; focusing on the sensations in your body without allowing your mind to interfere. And it's not limited to just sitting still with closed eyes. You can meditate while taking a walk, eating, or relaxing if you stay present with the sensations of your body.

The body communicates through sensations, which may seem boring compared to the mind's vivid images, sounds, and stories, but it's important to recognize that the body is more closely connected to reality. Embrace the sensations of your body and don't be discouraged by the lack of excitement, as this connection to reality is what truly matters.

One of the easiest ways to connect with your body is to focus on your breath. Observe your breath and pay attention to any sensations that arise in your body. Remember, if the sensation originates from your body, it's real, and if it originates from your mind, it's imagined. By staying with the physical sensations, you can stay grounded in reality and connect with the true essence of who you are.

So I should just experience the sensation and not categorize it as good or bad?

Being fully present in each moment is key to living in the present. Every moment offers a choice to either experience the moment or think about it, but not both at the same time. When we are fully engaged in the experience, there's no room for thoughts, and when we're thinking, we're not paying attention to the actual experience.

For instance, if I ask someone to sit and focus on a candle flame for a few moments, they'll have to choose between focusing on the flame or thinking about it. The difference between these two is subtle but significant. Every time they think about the candle flame, they're imagining its properties and characteristics in their mind. Reality is simple; it's just this moment, and everything else is a creation of the mind. The challenge of practicing mindfulness or meditation is to resist the mind's urge to intrude and block the body's perception of reality.

Regular practice of being present in each moment can help distinguish between the experiences of the mind and body. Trust the experiences of the body, as it has given us a deeper understanding of reality through physical sensations. Qualities like hardness and softness, light and darkness, sweetness and bitterness, beauty and ugliness, and pleasure and pain are all physical experiences. Unlike the mind, the body is not whimsical or fleeting. Its experiences have developed and matured over time, representing the wisdom we've gained from our interactions with the world.

The mind is like a roller coaster, constantly changing and unpredictable. On the other hand, the body is a rock-solid foundation that provides us with a stable connection to reality. The mind can be easily influenced by external and internal factors, making it difficult to control without the help of the body. This is why many meditation techniques focus on the body, using it as a starting point for our practice.

The word "Tantra" comes from the Sanskrit words "Tan," meaning "body," and "Tra," meaning "technique." Any meditation that focuses on the body can be considered a Tantric meditation. This includes practices like breathing meditation or "Vipassana." In contrast, meditation that focuses on the mind is referred to as Mantra meditation, coming from the roots "Man," meaning "mind," and "Tra," meaning "technique."

Chanting and focusing on one's thoughts are common in Mantra meditation, but it can be difficult for many people to sustain that level of focus. In comparison, meditating by focusing on the body is more accessible and easier for most people, making it a popular starting point for scientific meditation techniques. Whether it's focusing on the breath, forehead, heart center, or any other part of the body, the stability and reliability of the body offer a foundation for meditation and spiritual growth.

If you want to tap into the sensations of your body, just zero in on a specific spot on your body. There's no need to put too much pressure on making meditation happen, it'll come to you when it's meant to. Keep your focus sharp and be conscious of any thoughts trying to steer your attention away from the body. It can be tempting to wander into thoughts and miss the sensations, but with awareness and discipline, you can remain present with the physical experience.

For instance, if you're listening to the croaking of frogs near a pond, focus on the sensations in your body as you listen. Pay attention to how your body reacts to the sounds and concentrate on the experience instead of letting your mind wander into thoughts about the origin of the sound or the nature of frog calls. Once you start to think about these things, you've moved away from the body experience and into the mind and imagination.

By staying present with the body sensations, you can actually perceive all sounds as vibrations within your body. Close your eyes and try to feel the sounds by focusing on the sensations in your body, and you'll notice that your body is vibrating in sync with the sound. By staying present and avoiding distractions, you can experience a deeper connection between your body and the environment. There's a certain joy in being in nature and observing the sensations of your body. Unfortunately, we're slowly losing the ability to experience life through our bodies and becoming more and more consumed by our minds.

Have you ever stopped to really savor the sweet aroma of a blooming flower? When was the last time you fully embraced the feeling of the rain soaking into your skin and the earthy scent it brings? Have you recently taken a moment to sit in nature and let its beauty flow through you? Can you remember the last time you felt the sensation of walking barefoot on the grass, or truly focused on the rhythm of your breath? It's amazing how much of our lives we spend thinking about life rather than truly living it.

As you go deeper into mindfulness and meditation, it's important to be aware of the sensations in your body. This can give you a clearer and more tangible understanding of your connection to the world around you. By focusing on your body and its sensations, life can become more vivid and real. On the other hand, relying solely on your thoughts and mental experiences can lead to a confusing and disjointed perception of reality. Take a moment to reflect on your experiences throughout the day and ask yourself, "Is this a real physical experience that I should pay attention to through my body or just a fleeting thought in my mind that I can let go of?"

What about language? Is it an experience of the mind or the body?

As someone who's into mindfulness and meditation, it's important to understand the power of language and its connection to the mind. Our mind constantly communicates through language, and this internal dialogue is a clear indication of its presence. Language is a tool created by humans to articulate our thoughts, but it can also be used to manipulate and mislead others. It's easy to trick ourselves into limiting beliefs and self-imposed restrictions through the language we use to describe and understand the world around us.

On the other hand, the body has a more direct connection to reality and communicates through sensations that are much more straightforward than language. There is no such thing as "body language" as the body doesn't need symbolic representation to understand or interact with its environment. Trusting the signals from your body over the constantly changing thoughts of the mind is a wise choice. The body responds to reality through practice and experience, not language like the mind, and only gets better with repetition.

By focusing on the sensations of the body, such as the sensation of breathing, you can find a deeper sense of peace and stability than relying on the chatter of your mind. So, prioritize the signals from your body for a more grounded and peaceful life.

Beware of your mind

"My mind is like my browser: 19 tabs are open, 3 of them are frozen, and I have no idea where the music is coming from."

Anonymous

My mind is a constant chatter of thoughts. I mean, I can't stop the mind, and when I sit to meditate, my mind goes on overdrive; there's a song playing in the background, someone is there with a megaphone, and people are talking. How do I get them to shut up so that I can be still and meditate?

"My mind is a mess" is a phrase we often use, but it's not entirely accurate to just say the mind is chaotic. The mind is a much more complex phenomenon and the concept of noise or distractions is just one aspect of it. The idea of a "no-mind" state, as described in Buddhist philosophy, means a state of awareness that's free from the limitations of thoughts, emotions, and mental patterns. But this doesn't mean that the mind disappears when there are no thoughts. Instead, it still exists in its pure, undisturbed form.

To get a better understanding of the mind, it's important to examine it closely: what does it want, how does it work, and what's its intention? The mind is often seen as the boss of our thoughts and actions and it wants to keep that control. During meditation, when we try to quiet the mind, it may resist and try to stay in charge by creating thoughts and distractions. This internal dialogue, or noise, is what we need to be mindful of during meditation. The intention of meditation isn't to avoid this noise, but to understand it and get a deeper understanding of the mind. By observing the mind's behavior and motivations, we can gain a clearer perspective of the nature of the mind.

Not understanding the mind is what keeps it active. The more time we spend understanding the mind, the more peace and clarity we'll experience. The mind tends to operate in a state of confusion and it likes to stay elusive and unclear. Through meditation, we can shed light on the mind's behavior and motivations. It's like turning on the lights in a dark room - the mind, like a monster, can't stand the brightness and wants to hide. By observing the mind, its true nature is revealed and its grip on us lessens. Meditation helps one gain a deeper understanding of the mind, to have more control over their thoughts and actions.

Our thinking often involves going back and forth between memories and worries. When meditating, we observe this fluctuation without trying to change it. Over time, with practice, the frequency and intensity of these thoughts will decrease, and the mind will start to calm down. At first, the mind may wander during meditation, but with consistency, it will become more focused. The mind will still go back and forth, but the swings will become shorter and less intense. As the mind becomes more still, there will be fewer fluctuations, leading to a peaceful and calm state of mind. The goal of meditation is to bring the mind to a state of stillness, where it's not constantly swinging between thoughts and emotions.

Trying to control or suppress the mind with force will only lead to frustration and failure. The mind is designed to resist such attempts, and trying to fight it will only make it stronger. Telling the mind not to think about certain things during meditation will not work because it creates more thoughts and mental activity, which the mind enjoys. The key to calming the mind is to accept its fluctuation and allow it to settle down naturally. Over time, the mind will learn to find peace in the present moment. This process will take time, but you'll know it's happening when you start to experience a greater sense of peace and stillness. The goal of meditation is not to control the mind, but to observe it and let it find its natural state of calmness.

In simpler terms, it's crucial to understand that our mind is often linked to negative feelings like fear and anxiety, whereas our heart is associated with peace and positivity. If you're looking to find inner peace and see life from a fresh perspective, relying solely on your mind won't help. The deeper you delve into the mind, the more anxious and fearful you may become.

Instead, the practice of meditation will move your focus away from the mind's constant chatter, to focus on the heart. By shifting your attention to the heart, you can take control of your thoughts and emotions, and feel a deeper sense of peace and calmness. It's all about letting go of the mind's control and embracing a more heart-centered approach to life.

"One day Buddha was walking from one town to another with a few of his followers. While they were traveling, they passed a lake. They stopped and Buddha said to one of his disciples; "I am thirsty. Get me some water from that lake."

The disciple walked up to the lake. When he reached it, he noticed that some people were washing clothes in the water and, right at that moment, a bullock cart started crossing through the lake. As a result, the water became very muddy, very turbid. The disciple thought, "How can I give this muddy water to Buddha to drink?" So he came back and told Buddha, "The water is very muddy. I don't think it is fit to drink."

After about half an hour, again Buddha asked the same disciple to go back to the lake and get him some water to drink. The disciple obediently went back to the lake. This time he found that the lake had clear water in it. The mud had settled down and the water above it looked fit to collect. So he collected some water in a pot and brought it to Buddha.

Buddha looked at the water, and then he looked up at the disciple and said, "See what you did to make the water clean? You let it be ... and the mud settled down on its own and you got clear water... Your mind is also like that. When it is disturbed, just let it be. Give it a little time. It will settle down on its own. You don't have to put in an effort to calm it down. It will happen. It is effortless."

The mind has been the filter for all our experiences and actions up until now. Even when we try to approach life with love and an open heart, the mind can get in the way and block our true perception of reality. The mind is often filled with doubts and fears, such as "Love is dangerous" or "What if I get hurt again?" These thoughts are part of the mind's internal dialogue and can keep us from fully experiencing life.

The mind can be seen as a collection of all our fears and negative experiences, and we tend to store negative emotions there because there's nowhere else to put them. This is why meditation is so important; it helps us quiet the mind and gain a clearer understanding of our thoughts and emotions, so we can live life more fully with an open heart.

Meditation can be a challenging journey as it requires us to examine our past experiences and emotions in a new light. During meditation, we face the clutter, negativity, and unresolved emotions stored in our minds. Negative emotions and experiences can't be suppressed forever and will eventually come to the surface. Throughout our lives, we may have unconsciously accumulated unresolved emotions, desires, and experiences, leading to a cluttered mind.

When we first start meditating and observing the mind, it can be overwhelming and unsettling, as there are many thoughts, fears, and emotions vying for our attention. But this is precisely why meditation is so important; it helps us quiet the mind and find peace and clarity amidst life's chaos. By making meditation a regular practice, we can better manage our thoughts and emotions.

The mind has taken over our lives and overpowered our other senses. The mind is a useful tool, but it should be under our control. Imagine if our legs were constantly flopping around and we couldn't control them. In a similar way, the mind is always active, confrontational, and trying to do something. If we allow the mind to be in charge, our lives will be chaotic and difficult. But if we have control over the mind, we can use it as a tool when necessary. The goal of meditation is to gain control over the mind, so we can live a more peaceful and fulfilling life. By observing and understanding the mind, we can gain mastery over it and use it to our advantage, instead of being controlled by it.

When we let our minds run the show, our lives become a mess. We've been taught to believe that having more thoughts and reaching more goals equals happiness, but that's just not true. The mind is always searching for the next thing to make us happy, but once we get it, the cycle starts all over again. The mind creates desires and urges us to pursue them, leading to fear, frustration, and uncertainty. This is just how the mind operates - it's always scratching the wounds of the past and trying to find a solution in the future. But if we keep letting the mind control us, we'll never find true happiness. That's where meditation comes in - it helps us break this cycle and take control of our minds, so we can find peace and contentment in the present moment, instead of constantly chasing after what the mind desires.

Meditation is a unique process that lets you distinguish between your true self and the chaos of the mind. With meditation, you can control your mind and use it as a tool when necessary, and quiet it when you don't need it. As you get better at quieting your mind, you'll have access to new ways of perceiving the world, including intuition. Intuition is a powerful form of perception that can greatly improve your life, but it's often ignored in a world that values thinking and logic. But meditation can help you tap into your intuitive abilities by shifting your focus away from structured and repetitive thinking, and towards a more intuitive, creative and present-focused state of mind.

It's important to realize that the mind is all about repetition. It keeps repeating the same information over and over, even though it may seem like it's presenting something new. When we're stuck in our minds, it's hard to be creative or authentic. To tap into our true intuitive self, we need to break away from the mind's repetitive patterns.

In today's fast-paced world, we're missing one key component: the ability to truly experience life through our intuition. We've reduced life to just concepts and ideas, and have lost touch with the power of living in each moment. Instead, we rely on others' answers and become trapped in our own minds, spending our lives trying to rearrange our mental prison but never truly breaking free. That's why spirituality is so vital. It's the only path that can help us escape mental imprisonment and experience life to the fullest.

Spirituality is a deep-rooted yearning that arises within us when we're trapped by our minds. Meditation is a battle between the spirit and the mind; it's not just a man-made ideology or theory. The longing for stillness is a quest for the self to find true liberation and reach its highest purpose. Our thoughts have taken away our freedom, but meditation represents a path to liberation. Once you've tasted the true essence of meditation, you'll never let go. Your intuition will tell you that it's a way to escape the mind and all its fears, frustrations, and confusion.

NATURE OF THE MIND

"There is nothing more important to true growth than realizing that you are not the voice of the mind - you are the one who hears it."

Michael A. Singer

What is mind and what is existence, and what is the connection between the two?

According to the ancient Hindu beliefs, the mind is a vast and transcendental phenomenon. The word "man" or "mun" in Sanskrit means "mind" and is the root word for the English words "man" and "woman". Unlike modern thinking that the mind is generated in the brain, the ancient Hindus believed that the body was a manifestation of the mind and not the other way around. They believed in a higher creative force, referred to as "Brahman" or "The Vast Mind," that governed the human mind.

According to several ancient belief systems, each person is a creator as they possess the mind. In this view, an individual's reality is created through the process of perception, learning, and observation. Sounds, colors, textures, and desires are all aspects of the mind, and the mind is not considered a part of physical reality, but instead physical reality is regarded as a part of the mind.

The mind is essential for perception, experience, and the human journey. Without the mind, nothing would exist, and existence would be meaningless. Can you see the colors of a rainbow or the green of the trees without your mind? Can you have thoughts, desires, or experiences without the mind? The answer is no. The mind is necessary for our existence and the human journey. So, consider the question, "What is not the mind?" The answer may surprise you.

When you believe your mind is disturbed, just remember it's not the mind itself that's disturbed, but the disturbance has been added to it. The mind, as an entity, is always the same, regardless of its content. The ancient Hindus believed that there is only one mind - the perceiving mind, the observing mind, and that everything in existence is part of this mind. They divided the mind into compartments and referred to it by different names, but in essence, it's still the same mind. So, when we say "My mind is restless," "My mind is fearful," or "My mind is quiet," we are referring to the content of the mind, not the mind itself.

Think of your mind like a cup. The cup itself doesn't have any qualities, but based on what you pour into it, you assign qualities to it. If you pour water into the cup, it will accept it. If you pour coffee into it, it will accept it too. The cup doesn't question its contents. It accepts things unconditionally. If the mind is not interested in understanding its contents, then who's talking about a disturbed mind or a peaceful mind? Who's on this quest to understand the mind?

To calm the mind, distractions like watching a movie or keeping busy won't work. You need a different approach, and that approach is meditation. Meditation is a scientific method for understanding the mind that is everywhere yet invisible. So, the next time you feel that your mind is disturbed, instead of seeking distractions, try meditating.

There are only two things that truly exist - the mind and what it is focused on. Right now, part of your mind is focused on you - your appearance, your behavior, your identity, and your aspirations. But, when you let go of this focus on the visible self, you'll understand the truth. Spirituality is all about letting go of the ego, and it's not possible to be spiritual while holding onto a false ego. As you continue on your spiritual journey, you'll slowly let go of your attachment to the false ego.

Now, what exactly is the ego? Is it a real entity? Well, it's important to understand that our thoughts, mind, and body are real, but the ego is not. The ego is just a false attachment to the body and mind, a self-made wall that provides a false sense of security. Our name, fame, and wealth are all part of the ego. Meditation is a way to break down these walls. Some people may be hesitant to try meditation because they're afraid of losing their mind, but that's not the case.

The instructions for meditation can be confusing, with phrases like "drop your mind" and "drop your body." It's understandable if these instructions are unsettling, as they seem to suggest giving up something precious and essential. You might be thinking, "Why would I want to drop my mind? That's all I have. And my body, that's my life! I love my life. Can you teach me something to help me relax, but what do you mean, drop the body?"

But, even if you reach the deepest levels of meditation, you won't lose your body or mind. Instead, you'll let go of the false identification with your body and the false identification with your mind. This way, you'll come to understand that there's a third aspect to your reality that exists beyond the mind and body. You are not the mind, the body, or the ego - you are something else entirely.

When you experience the pure moment of being something different, your attachment to the body and mind will naturally fade away. This is known as the moment of enlightenment. Your body and mind will still be there, but the desire to cling to them will be gone. Only the false ego will have disappeared, and that's all that needs to happen.

Enlightenment is not a new experience, but rather a realization of your true self. At that moment of realization, you'll understand what the mind is. The mind is your center and cannot be discarded. You can quiet the mind by clearing your thoughts, but you can never escape the mind because everything exists within it. The mind has no boundaries and extends to the edges of space and the universe. Meditation is not about escaping the mind, but rather understanding its true nature.

Enlightenment is not about giving up or transcending anything, but rather, it is a transformative experience in which you become everything. It's the realization that you have always been where you were meant to be and that you didn't have to change yourself or move somewhere to achieve enlightenment. In this state, you understand that you are the mind, and the mind is you, without any limitations or boundaries. Since everything is a part of the mind, there's no need for any movement within it. Enlightenment is about accepting the present moment as complete reality and understanding that it is already whole and perfect. It represents a shift from a constructed, limited mind to the eternal, infinite mind.

As a human, it's easy to get caught up in the hustle and bustle of life and all the things we've created - the buildings, the businesses, the lifestyle. But if you take a step back and immerse yourself in nature, you'll see the difference between the "human mind" and the "mind." The peaceful and serene environment of nature is a stark contrast to the busy and structured city. Existence is complete and beautiful, and it's not driven by any specific purpose. The animals, the trees, the sky - they all just exist for their own sake.

Existence itself is not purpose-driven, but when we use our human intelligence to create things with specific purposes, like building a home or a chair, that's when the human mind comes into play. But it's important to remember that existence itself is simply what it is, without any purpose. And sometimes, it's good to return to that unstructured space of the mind, where everything just exists for its own sake.

The Silent Path

Spirituality in the modern world

"We are not human beings having a spiritual experience. We are spiritual beings having a human experience."

Pierre Teilhard de Chardin

Why would I want to pursue a spiritual path if I had a good job, a family, a car, a house, and everything else I needed? What is the reason to follow a spiritual path, and how can I accommodate a spiritual way of life in my already materialistic lifestyle?

Material possessions like a big house, a fancy car, and a well-paying job might give us a false sense of security and comfort, but they do not bring lasting happiness. In fact, the more we accumulate, the more we realize that something is missing, both in our lives and within us. So, it's important to understand that true happiness comes from within and can only be achieved through self-discovery and spiritual growth.

Many people, in their quest for success, forget about their spiritual well-being and ignore the importance of introspection. But true success in life is not just about acquiring external wealth and achievements, but also about knowing who you are and what your purpose in life is. Those who prioritize their spiritual growth tend to find more joy and fulfillment in life, as they have a clearer sense of their true selves.

It's important to understand that the meaning of life can only be found when we look inward and not just focus on external appearances. We should not compare ourselves to others or try to prove our intelligence or strength, as this only takes us away from our true selves. In the end, what truly matters is our personal growth and understanding of who we are and what we want to achieve in life.

In this fast-paced world, it's easy to look around and feel like everyone else is doing better than you. With new technology and advancements happening every day, it can feel like your accomplishments are becoming obsolete and even unimportant. But it's important to remember that true success and happiness come from within. That's where spirituality comes in.

Spirituality is all about understanding who you truly are and focusing on self-care and well-being. It's not about approaching it with religious fervor or ignoring it completely. It's a journey of self-discovery and realizing that you are the center of your own life and that everything else takes a backseat.

By delving into the inner world and organizing the mess of experiences in our minds and bodies, we can gain a better understanding of the purpose and significance of our lives. Spirituality is about bringing order to the core of our existence and finding everything we need within ourselves.

However, if you're willing to make some adjustments to your routine, you can definitely find time for spirituality. For instance, reducing your sleep time and using the extra hours for meditation is a great place to start. Meditation is a form of rest for the body and can even lead to needing less sleep. By becoming more mindful and introspective through meditation, you can boost your productivity and avoid wasting time in your daily routine.

Incorporating spirituality into your life can also bring a sense of calm and peace, even amidst the chaos of daily life. This can help you handle stress and challenges in a more positive and productive way.

Remember, spirituality is a personal journey, and there is no right or wrong way to go about it. The most important thing is to listen to your own inner voice and let your intuition guide you. Your spiritual path should bring joy and fulfillment to your life, and not become an added source of stress. So, make sure to find a balance that works for you, and always prioritize your well-being above everything else.

It's essential to understand that the pursuit of material wealth and survival is not the same as the pursuit of spirituality and self-discovery. The former is based on external factors, such as societal norms and expectations, while the latter is based on an internal journey of self-awareness and growth.

Spirituality is about finding your own truth, discovering your purpose in life, and creating a sense of inner peace and fulfillment. It's a journey of self-discovery, one that requires time, patience, and persistence. It can be challenging, but the rewards are immeasurable. By finding your own truth and purpose, you'll be able to lead a life that is authentic, meaningful, and fulfilling.

In the end, it's up to each individual to decide what their priorities are. Some may choose to focus on material wealth, while others may choose spirituality. But, it's important to remember that our lives are finite, and the choices we make now will shape the rest of our journey. By prioritizing spirituality and self-discovery, we can create a life that is full of purpose and meaning, one that will be remembered long after we're gone.

Spirituality requires a deep understanding of our own selves and the world around us. It's not just about practicing religion or following a certain set of beliefs, but rather, it's about discovering the truth within ourselves. By focusing on what truly matters and prioritizing our own well-being, we can find a sense of peace and fulfillment that cannot be achieved through material success alone.

True wealth is not just about what we have in terms of material possessions, but rather, it's about recognizing the abundance in our lives. This includes acknowledging our own strengths and abilities, as well as the support and love we receive from others. When we understand our own worth and have a deep appreciation for what we have, we become less reliant on external sources for security and happiness.

The pursuit of spirituality requires a level of trust in ourselves and the unknown. It's important to recognize that life isn't completely in our control and there's more to it than just our own efforts. By embracing uncertainty and letting go of the need for control, we can find peace and contentment in the present moment.

Pursuing spirituality and understanding life is a lifelong journey that requires dedication and a willingness to change. By prioritizing self-discovery and recognizing the riches within, we can find true wealth and fulfillment in life, regardless of our material possessions or circumstances.

Embarking on a spiritual journey requires a bold step of faith, like taking a leap into the unknown with full trust in yourself. The moment we fully trust ourselves is the moment of spiritual liberation. The rest of the journey is realizing that we have already found what we were searching for. We don't become spiritual through a lengthy quest, but rather in the moment we choose to fully trust ourselves.

If you want to access your inner spirit, you must be willing to let go of anything that is holding you back. This means freeing yourself from societal expectations, your own thoughts and emotions, and deep attachment to material possessions you've accumulated. This moment of pure liberation opens up a world of endless possibilities. However, it takes bravery to get there.

It's important to note that spirituality and religion are two separate concepts. Religion says that you need someone else to save you, while spirituality says that you have the power to save yourself. It's about relying on your own intelligence, self-awareness, and understanding of life, instead of seeking answers from outside sources.

Embarking on a spiritual journey is a personal journey of self-discovery. It's not about conforming to someone else's beliefs or following a set of rules. It's about finding your own connection with the universe and creating your own path. So, don't be afraid to go against the grain and find what resonates with you.

Asking the big questions of life - "Who am I?" and "What's my purpose?" - is the first step towards spirituality. The journey may not be easy, and you may face opposition from those around you. But if you're willing to endure the process of self-discovery, the answers will come.

Meditation plays a significant role in this journey. It's an opportunity to calm the mind, reflect on your thoughts and emotions, and peel away the layers that don't belong to your true self. Over time, you'll start to uncover your authentic self and understand what's important to hold onto and what to let go of.

And never forget, material wealth cannot replace the pursuit of self-discovery and understanding of life. The universe supports you on your spiritual journey, so have the courage to take that leap of faith and uncover your true self.

The path to spirituality begins when you can find peace and contentment in your own company. This is the moment when you break away from the limitations imposed by your mind, body, society, and possessions. The liberation that comes with this realization opens up a world of new possibilities. However, it takes courage to take that first step, as it's not always easy to let go of what we're used to.

In spirituality, you rely on your own intelligence, awareness, and understanding of life, instead of relying on external sources. When you make this shift, you can balance your material desires with your spiritual quest. To make spirituality a part of your life, you need to integrate it into your daily routine and make it a habit, not just a one-off activity. Your lifestyle must be adjusted to accommodate your spiritual journey, not the other way around.

Life is not predetermined. Just because you were born into a certain family, have certain physical attributes, or have material wealth, it doesn't guarantee a fulfilling life. You are only given the opportunity of life, and what you make of it is entirely up to you. Think of your life as a sculptor carving a piece of marble, which represents you. Chisel away all the external influences and accumulated baggage to reveal your true self. The perfect version of you already exists within the marble, and all that needs to be removed is the unwanted stuff.

Michelangelo was once asked how he was able to make such stunning sculptures with great body proportions. He answered, "The statue is already there within the block of marble, I just need to chip away the excess." Similarly, we are like a piece of marble when we are born, a part of life. To live a life that's truly fulfilling, we need to have a clear vision of who we want to be and work towards becoming that person. Many of us go through life without a clear idea of who we are, simply going through the motions, hoping to eventually discover our true selves. Spirituality involves seeing ourselves as a perfect being and striving to become that. Even though we are already perfect as we are, we need to let go of the things that hold us back from experiencing our inner perfection. This is why spirituality requires a leap of faith, as we need to trust in our own vision and ability to make it a reality.

When starting a spiritual journey, you may feel alone, as not many people focus on introspection. It's common for your mind to question your choices and compare them to those who are content with external pleasures. Your mind may even doubt your path and tell you, "You're the only one on this journey, and you're lost." But it's crucial to have the bravery to stay strong and not give in to these thoughts. You need to reassure your mind by saying, "It's okay, I'm taking this time to understand myself, and everything else will follow." No one who has begun a spiritual journey has ever regretted it.

The spiritual path is unique to each individual and cannot be replicated. Following a specific religion or belief system may not align with one's personal beliefs and values. Blindly following a religion is like trying to wear someone else's coat, which may not fit properly. In spirituality, there's no one solution that fits everyone. Each person must create their own understanding and relationship with their spirituality. This personal connection cannot be imposed on others.

When we ask questions like, "Who am I, where did I come from, and what's the purpose of my life?" we are exploring ourselves and life itself. This is when we begin our spiritual journey. Spirituality is not an easy path. We may not receive support from friends and family, and we may even lose some people along the way. Each obstacle is painful, but we must endure it, as we are sculpting ourselves and there's no avoiding the process. Our emotions, thoughts, identity, and self-image must be shaped from the chaos of life. It takes time and effort, but if we're not willing to endure the pain, we'll never find answers to life's most important questions. We may have a safe and secure life, but what's the point if we don't know who we are?

Meditation is an integral part of the spiritual journey. It allows you to peel away the things that are not truly you, like thoughts, emotions, and beliefs, and get to the core of who you truly are. Over time, your true self will start to emerge, and you'll become aware of the things you need to hold onto and the things you need to let go of.

Material wealth can't replace the quest for self-discovery and a deeper understanding of life. Asking the big questions about life and exploring spirituality is important, and those who seek answers will eventually find them. You're never alone on this journey, as the entire universe is supporting you. Spirituality is not just about knowing yourself, but also about understanding everything around you.

ACCEPTING YOURSELF

"We have to dare to be ourselves, however frightening
or strange that self may prove to be."

May Sarton

**Why is there a constant internal conflict? Why
am I unable to accept myself fully? Can
meditation help with this?**

Our emotions can be a rollercoaster, constantly
shifting between joy, sadness, frustration, and
disappointment. These emotions are often driven by
external factors, our expectations, and how we react
to them. While we can't completely control our
emotions, it's important to be mindful of them before
making any decisions. Negative emotions can cloud
our judgment and lead to regretful actions.

Meditation is a powerful tool for managing our
emotions, as it provides a space for stillness and
calmness. By practicing meditation regularly, we can

gain a better understanding and control of our emotions, leading to more mindful and intentional decision-making.

Mindfulness is also an important aspect of emotional balance and well-being. Incorporating mindfulness into our daily lives, such as taking a mindful walk, can greatly enhance our experiences and perspectives. Instead of letting your thoughts wander, focus on the present moment and pay attention to the present. By being mindful, you can find peace and reduce anxiety, fear, and frustration caused by excessive thoughts and worries.

Meditation is not just for those struggling with issues such as anxiety or stress, but it's a tool for anyone who wants to find mental wellness and inner peace. It's a common misconception that meditation is only necessary if something is wrong, but in reality, it's a means to maintain and improve your mental health even if everything is going well.

Daily life can bring about stress, worries, and distractions, and meditation helps to calm the mind and bring peace. Regular practice of meditation can reveal its many benefits, and those who experience its transformative effects often become its enthusiastic proponents. Buddha himself spent 40 years teaching about meditation after his enlightenment, emphasizing its importance for mental well-being. So, don't wait for something to be wrong before trying meditation. Embrace it as a tool for personal growth and self-discovery, and experience the peace and calm it can bring to your mind.

Meditation helps us accept and understand our emotions, including those that we may perceive as negative. For example, if anger is a tendency, the more we can accept and understand this aspect of our personality, the less we'll feel the need to get angry. Anger often stems from an internal struggle where the root cause is unclear. Meditation provides a space for self-reflection and understanding, allowing us to embrace and accept our emotions, rather than fighting against them. This can help reduce feelings of inner turmoil and promote greater self-acceptance.

It's important to understand that meditation doesn't restrict or take away one's ability to experience emotions. It's not about suppressing emotions but about being more mindful and intentional in how we respond to them. So, don't have unrealistic expectations when you first start practicing meditation. It's not a quick fix but a tool to help us better understand ourselves and our emotions.

Through meditation we can cultivate self-love and acceptance, as it trains us to observe our emotions without being fully consumed by them. Instead of denying or suppressing negative emotions like anger, meditation encourages us to recognize and embrace them, and make conscious choices about whether or not to express them. This shift in perspective leads to greater emotional control and well-being.

Meditation is the practice of letting go of attachment to emotions, whether they be positive or negative. During meditation, we become the observer of our thoughts and emotions, instead of being fully identified with them. By acknowledging and accepting emotions as temporary experiences, rather than defining ourselves by them, we can develop a sense of detachment and equanimity, allowing us to better navigate life's ups and downs.

True happiness comes from the ability to observe and acknowledge life's experiences and emotions, while remaining detached from them. Regular meditation can help us develop the skills necessary to manage emotions in a more mindful and intentional way. It's important to remember that limiting beliefs, such as the idea that a happy person shouldn't experience negative emotions, can hold us back from experiencing true happiness. Emotions, including anger, are a natural part of life and can be experienced without detracting from overall happiness. The issue is not the presence of anger, but a lack of acceptance and understanding of it.

Meditation allows you to embrace all parts of yourself, including your emotions and experiences, without judgment. Society often perpetuates the idea that happiness is the only desirable state, but this notion can limit personal growth and lead to feelings of inadequacy. True wisdom and growth come from accepting all aspects of oneself, including the difficulties and challenges in life, with equanimity.

Helping you see your thoughts and emotions with clarity, meditation provides a space for self-awareness. It doesn't see emotions or actions as flawed or in need of correction, but rather offers an opportunity for understanding without judgment. By embracing a mindful, non-judgmental approach, meditation helps you develop a deeper understanding of yourself and the world around you.

The key to happiness is not holding onto it, but accepting and embracing all emotions, even those that may be perceived as negative. True wisdom comes from recognizing that life is not solely made up of happiness, but also includes fear, frustration, and other difficulties. Meditation helps you understand and navigate all of your experiences, without trying to avoid or suppress any part of yourself. Empower yourself to make conscious choices and find fulfillment through self-awareness and illumination.

The truth is, life is too short to waste time trying to change every aspect of ourselves to fit society's standards. We have a choice to make: we can either embrace who we are, flaws and all, and celebrate our unique qualities, or we can spend our lives fighting against our own beliefs of what's right and wrong. When we learn to accept ourselves just as we are, the change we desire comes naturally and with ease. The more we embrace our individuality, the less inner turmoil we experience, leading to greater peace and happiness.

Society often sets strict definitions of what it means to be a good person or what's considered right and wrong, but these narrow views don't allow for the individuality and complexity of each person. To preserve our uniqueness and beauty, it's crucial to practice self-awareness through tools like meditation. Meditation isn't about following a certain set of beliefs or religious teachings, it's a universal tool for understanding and exploring our own lives. By using this tool, we can break free from societal expectations and live life on our own terms.

Starting a meditation practice can be intimidating because there's no one there to guide us. But, this lack of structure also gives us complete freedom in meditation. We're left alone with our mind and body, free to explore and understand them in a new way. Meditation encourages a personal approach, rather than an intellectual or philosophical one. The focus is on simply being in the present moment, rather than striving to become something specific. This freedom can feel overwhelming at first, but with time, you'll learn to trust the process and tap into the transformative power of meditation.

In other words, embracing an existential outlook means being mindful and accepting of each moment as it is, without trying to change or control it. Instead of trying to hide from or alter our emotions, like anger, we simply acknowledge them and allow them to pass. This idea is at the core of meditation, which encourages us to observe our experiences with a non-judgmental perspective. By letting go of the need to control our emotions or experiences, we can trust that growth and change will happen naturally. This shift towards mindfulness and acceptance can bring a greater sense of peace and contentment to our lives.

MEDITATION

"When you connect to the silence within you, that is when you can make sense of the disturbance going on around you."

Stephen Richards

You said that meditation is not easy, and to get the most from meditation you should put yourself into more difficult situations to make meditation more difficult, like meditating late at night. But after a certain point, it's just too difficult, so how do you find that balance?

Meditation is a practice that requires effort, but not in the traditional sense. Keeping your mind and body still, focused, and relaxed can be a challenge, especially with the constant barrage of thoughts and distractions. But, the key to making progress in meditation lies in finding the right balance between ease and effort.

It's important to understand that meditation is not just about sitting down and letting go of everything. While you want to relax and find peace, it takes effort to maintain focus and keep your mind from wandering. It's a constant battle between your habits, upbringing, past experiences, and the present moment.

When you're trying to meditate, it can feel like you're putting in a lot of effort. This is completely normal, especially if you're used to living a busy and active lifestyle. Your past experiences and habits can have a significant impact on your mind and body, and it can be difficult to break away from them. For instance, if you're trying to meditate right before your bedtime, you may find it tough to stay awake and focused. Your body may be used to winding down and preparing for sleep, but it's important to put in the effort to stay alert and resist the urge to doze off.

A student went to his meditation teacher and said, "My meditation is horrible! I feel so distracted, my legs ache, and I'm constantly falling asleep. It's just horrible!"

"It will pass," the teacher said matter-of-factly.

A week later, the student came back to his teacher. "My meditation is wonderful! I feel so aware, so peaceful, so alive! It's just wonderful!'

"It will pass," the teacher replied matter-of-factly.

There are two types of effort when it comes to meditation. The conscious effort you put in to deepen your meditation, and the effort needed to go beyond your mental and physical conditioning. For instance, if you decide to sit on the floor without a cushion or backrest, you may find it uncomfortable at first because your body is not conditioned to sit in that position. However, with consistent practice, you can train your body to become more comfortable in that position. It's essential to use your own judgment and ask yourself, "Do I really need to sit on the floor?" If the answer is no, then it's perfectly fine to sit on a chair or any other comfortable seat and still meditate effectively.

The goal of meditation is not to maintain a rigid, statue-like posture. The traditional meditation posture often depicted in art and literature can be misleading, making people believe that they must sit in a specific way to meditate. This misconception is largely due to the popular image of the sitting Buddha. However, the truth is that the posture of meditation is not fixed and can vary. If Buddha had chosen to sit with his hands clasped behind his head, that could have become a famous meditation posture, and people would have created stories to support it.

The notion that the lotus posture is unique and provides specific benefits, is similar to other misconceptions surrounding meditation postures. Buddha simply adopted the cross-legged sitting position on the floor with arms on his lap because it was comfortable for him and natural in his culture.

The most crucial factor in determining a meditation posture is finding a position in which you can comfortably relax your body without falling asleep. Postures that are too comfortable can induce sleep, taking you away from meditation. The ideal meditation posture is one in which you are both relaxed and alert. If you feel uncomfortable, you can make small adjustments to your position, but if you fall asleep, you are no longer meditating.

Meditation may seem like a passive activity, but in reality, it's quite active. Throughout the day, our mind and body are in constant motion, but when we try to sit still and meditate, the mind becomes active. If you observe your daily routine, you'll notice that both your mind and body are only briefly at rest. For instance, when you are working at a desk, your body is resting, but your mind is active. On the other hand, when you are running, your mind is not consumed by complicated thoughts, but your body is highly active.

Now, think about those times when you have been fully engaged in a mentally demanding task. Afterward, you might feel the need to go for a walk or get some exercise. In these moments, you are giving rest to your mind by making your body more active. Throughout the day, we tend to exert either our mind or our body, but in meditation, we learn how to keep both our mind and body at rest simultaneously.

This can be challenging because we have never experienced both our mind and body at rest while still being fully conscious and awake. That's why meditation requires effort and practice.

It's important to understand that the body and mind are not separate entities but rather a single extension of energy. When we focus energy on the mind, the body rests, and when we focus energy on the body, the mind rests. However, when both the body and mind are given equal amounts of energy, it creates a state of chaos.

We must be cautious of individuals who are exerting both their mind and body simultaneously, as they may not be in control of either. However, through meditation, we can learn to keep our mind and body at rest simultaneously, which creates a state of deep inner peace and tranquility. By achieving this state, we can experience a profound sense of relaxation and mental clarity.

Meditation can be easy and enjoyable at times, but it can also be disturbing or agitating. During those challenging moments, it's important to stay present and not give up on your meditation practice. To identify the cause of the disturbance, use your understanding of your mind and body. If your body is agitated, try to relax and adjust your posture for comfort. If your mind is causing the disturbance, choose a simple focus such as your breath or a mantra to redirect your thoughts.

Often, our minds become disturbed during meditation after a difficult conversation or deep thinking. If something has captured our attention, our mind will continue to wander in that direction during meditation. Practicing mindfulness throughout the day can help us to be more relaxed during meditation. If we are not mindful, our mind may continue to think about mundane tasks instead of being fully present in the moment. Mindfulness is the art of being in the present moment, and it requires daily practice.

How exactly do I begin my meditation practice?

To begin your meditation, start with full awareness. Find a comfortable position and close your eyes. Remind yourself that your goal is not to relax, but to observe any disturbances. Observe the discomfort of sitting, the effort involved, any physical pain, and the sensations in your body. By doing this, you become aware of both the mental and physical disturbances and simply observe them without judgment.

As you begin your meditation, you will notice your mind constantly trying to engage you in conversation. It may ask why you are in this position, what you should think about now, or why you are not sleeping. To quiet your mind, gently remind yourself to focus on your breath and ask your mind to be quiet for a moment.

However, just because your mind has become quiet does not necessarily mean you are relaxing and experiencing peace. It could mean that you are falling asleep. A quiet mind does not always equal a peaceful mind. If you become aware that your mind is becoming quiet and you are not experiencing any disturbances, make a conscious effort to stay awake by increasing your level of alertness and awareness.

The mind can appear quiet when it wanders, but this is different from having a meditative mind. The mind seems silent because it is lost in thought and you become gradually drowsy. To achieve a meditative state, you must be aware of your mind's continuous chatter and observe it without succumbing to sleep. The mind is like a radio that constantly plays, from the moment of birth until we find the off switch. The goal of meditation is to find that switch and quiet the mind.

Meditation is about creating balance between the energies of the mind and body. Although we may be physically present while meditating, our mind tends to wander. We must make a consistent effort to bring our attention back to the body. Each time we forget to focus on staying present, the mind drifts into thought. It can be a pleasant experience because the mind becomes calm and relaxed, but we may not realize that we've drifted into sleep and stopped paying attention. At the end of the meditation we may feel peaceful, but in reality, meditation is recognized by the presence of disturbance. If your meditation was not challenging, it is possible that you were asleep for most of it.

The purpose of meditation is not to avoid thoughts but to fully embrace them. Conflict fuels thoughts. When we accept a thought, it becomes less powerful than a thought we reject. The more we resist our thoughts, the more intense they become. Our thoughts continue to cycle with the energy given by our resistance to them. It's crucial for meditators to understand the nature of their thoughts. When we acknowledge and accept a thought, it gradually loses its power. In meditation, relaxation comes from accepting more and more of our conflicting thought processes and becoming comfortable with them. A relaxed mind is still filled with thoughts, but isn't disturbed.

The goal of meditation is not to eradicate thoughts but to bring them into the light of consciousness. Thoughts thrive in the darkness of the mind, where they can change and evolve without our knowledge. Awareness is the greatest challenge to a thought. When we become aware of our thoughts, they lose their power over us. Having many thoughts is not inherently wrong. The real disturbance comes from thoughts that go unnoticed. Meditation is about illuminating the mind, not purifying it. The objective is not to leave the mind empty but to make us fully aware of our thoughts. A thought that is observed can be a helpful tool, but an unnoticed thought is simply a distraction.

Meditation is about observing the disturbance of the mind, and relaxation is a result of observing and accepting our thoughts. This process takes time, patience, and consistent practice. Eventually, the mind and body become quiet, allowing for a moment of clarity and heightened awareness. It is then that our true self can awaken to a different reality.

The difference between being awake and asleep is finding balance between the extremes of the mind and body. Buddha taught that the middle path is not about avoiding the extremes of life, but avoiding the extremes of the mind and body. It is about finding a balance between keeping the mind alert enough to remain awake and keeping the body relaxed enough to be present in the moment. Buddha taught only one method for achieving this balance: "watching the breath."

Focusing on the breath is a fundamental aspect of meditation. By directing our attention to the breath, we can gain insight into the workings of our minds and bodies. It is a conscious effort that helps us understand the functioning of the mind. During meditation, the mind may question your intentions, and it may even analyze the act of focusing on the breath instead of actually focusing on it. It is essential to be aware of this and not to get caught up in the thoughts. Instead, we should come back to the breath and observe our thoughts objectively.

Meditation is not about controlling or suppressing thoughts; it's about observing them. When we watch the breath, we notice that the mind tends to wander, and it may try to analyze our actions. This is normal, and we should not get discouraged or judge ourselves for it. With regular practice, we can develop the necessary understanding and confidence to quiet the mind, and our meditation will become more effortless and peaceful. The primary objective of watching the breath during meditation is to bring awareness to the present moment. The breath serves as an anchor to keep the mind from wandering, allowing us to cultivate a calm, alert state where both the mind and body are at rest. It's not about finding answers to questions or solving problems, but about being fully present and aware of the present moment.

Understanding the complex nature of the mind is critical in finding inner peace and calm. Our mind is a constant flow of thoughts, emotions, and opinions shaped by our experiences, likes, dislikes, and fears. Shifting our focus from the realm of thoughts to a neutral state, like the breath, is essential in learning how to tame the mind. During meditation, it's important to keep the body relaxed and the mind alert through awareness and mindfulness to remain present in the moment and avoid succumbing to the agitation of the mind.

Meditation involves being mindful of your actions and being present in the moment. It's not about changing your habits, thoughts, or behavior but observing them as they are. By embracing the chaos of daily life and remaining mindful of your thoughts, clarity will arise. In fact, with consistent mindfulness practice throughout the day, meditation will occur naturally. When you sit down to meditate after an hour of being mindful, you'll notice how much easier it becomes to remain quiet and centered during your meditation. Meditation is simply a more concentrated form of mindfulness and the primary goal is to observe your thoughts. With consistent mindfulness practice, observing your thoughts during meditation will become more effortless and efficient.

Being a meditator is not limited to the time you spend sitting with your eyes closed. Meditation should be a continuous state of observation and mindfulness throughout the day. Buddha taught that if you can watch your thoughts for one hour without interruption, you will attain Enlightenment. This level of focus and awareness can only be achieved through the habit of observing your thoughts throughout the day. Your meditation practice is impacted by what you do during the day because you are one continuous being. The more aware you are during the day, the deeper you can go in meditation.

Our actions shape our identity, and unconscious actions become a part of us, influencing our thoughts and emotions. Traumatic experiences that occurred while we were not fully aware can be difficult to move beyond because they are deeply embedded in our identity. With increased awareness, we can separate the experiences of the mind, body, and self, and distinguish between what happened to us and who we are. By cultivating mindfulness throughout the day, we can observe our actions and thoughts more objectively, allowing us to let go of those experiences that no longer serve us.

It's important to remember that you are not defined by everything that happens to your mind and body. Awareness is a powerful tool to help you separate yourself from your experiences and avoid carrying their weight on your shoulders. When you collect and form your identity around every experience, life can become overwhelming. Whether it's positive or negative, each experience can weigh you down over time. Without awareness, it's easy to lose sight of the present moment and get caught up in the past or future.

Through regular practice of mindfulness and meditation, you can develop the ability to remain present and aware in every moment. Eventually, you may realize that there is no distinction between your sitting meditation and your walking meditation. You may find that you are in a meditative state all the time, and that you can experience a sense of bliss and beauty in every moment, without having to sit or close your eyes. This level of awareness can help you find a sense of peace and clarity, even in the midst of chaos or difficulty.

Meditation is not limited to a specific time or place. It is a way of being present and aware in every moment. To truly experience this, it's necessary to transform everything you observe into a meditative state. By becoming aware of the observer and the object being observed, you can integrate the experience into your being. This creates a sense of oneness, where everything is within you, and you are within everything.

For example, when you walk mindfully, you can feel the ground beneath your feet and the air on your skin. By fully experiencing the act of walking, it becomes a part of you. With practice, you can do this with everything - the breath, the sun, the trees, and more. By bringing everything within you, you can let go of the sense of separation that causes pain and confusion. When everything is within you, there is nothing left to seek or search for, and you can experience a sense of oneness with the world around you.

The pursuit of spirituality begins with a focus on self-reflection. To advance spiritually, it is necessary to concentrate on your own personal growth rather than the growth of others. Only your own life can be observed and analyzed, and it is important to have a keen interest in learning about yourself. While you may express love and kindness to others, you cannot force them to develop their own spiritual journey. Each individual must take their own initiative in this regard.

At the core of spirituality lies self-interest. To advance spiritually, you must prioritize your own self-reflection and development. Instead of trying to influence others, you must first examine and reform your own behavior and habits. For instance, if you learn that consuming meat is harmful to the environment, begin by making changes in your own diet rather than expecting others to follow suit. The key to spiritual growth is to practice self-reflection and self-improvement, while also extending unconditional love to others. Consistent meditation practice can help internalize the wisdom gained from the external world and form a strong foundation for your spiritual journey.

The Silent Path

FOCUS AND AWARENESS

"We all operate on different levels of awareness. Half the time I don't know what I'm doing."

Sebastian Faulks

How should we be observing the breath in our meditation practice? Should we be thinking about the breath, focusing on the breath, or have a periphery awareness of the breath, as if it is in the background?

In order to observe something effectively, you should have a clear understanding of what you want to observe. The same goes for observing the breath during meditation. The concept of "breath" needs to be defined in order to observe it properly. The challenge with observation is not with the act of observing, but with the lack of clarity in defining the object of observation. With a clear definition, observing becomes much easier.

When observing your breath, you need to recognize that your breath is not a single moment, but a continuous cycle. It starts as air from the outside, reaches your nostrils, enters your body, pauses for a moment, and then exits. It is not a single point, but a complete process. Understanding the difference between focus and awareness is crucial here. Instead of simply focusing on the breath, define the breath by focusing on a specific aspect, such as the air reaching your nostrils, the pause between breaths, or the contraction and expansion of your abdomen.

The key to successful meditation is to maintain full awareness on the process of breathing, rather than just focusing on one aspect. When in doubt, remember that as long as you are fully aware of your breath, you are meditating. By applying the principle of inquiry to your breath, you can achieve a clearer understanding of the object of observation, leading to a more focused and successful meditation practice.

While focus involves directing your attention to a single point, awareness involves being conscious of multiple things simultaneously. Archery requires focus, while meditation requires awareness. Focus is just the starting point of meditation, as it eventually evolves into the ability to simply be aware. When an archer is focused on the target and pulling back on the bowstring, they may not be aware of their surroundings. All their attention is consumed by their focus on the target. However, awareness is different as it does not consume all of your attention. When starting meditation, it can be challenging to simply be aware of things, so it's easier to start by focusing on a single point. With practice, this focus will expand into a broader state of awareness.

There is a famous story in ancient Hindu scriptures of Arjuna and his teacher Drona:

> Drona placed a wooden bird on a tree and brought his students 100 yards away. He instructed them not to fire their arrows until he told them to. He called up the first student and asked, "What do you see?" The student replied, "I see the tree, the bird, you, and everyone else." Drona told the student to keep looking, but they saw nothing else, so he sent them away. This process was repeated with several other students, but they all had the same result. When it was Arjuna's turn, Drona asked, "What do you see?" Arjuna,

standing in front of the tree, replied, "I see the eye of the bird." Drona then said, "Shoot," and Arjuna shot the arrow, hitting the bird directly in its eye.

This story teaches the importance of focus. Focus should be singular and narrow, accompanied by a strong determination to observe only what you have selected. There should be no confusion while focusing, as confusion indicates a lack of focus. The determination to focus is more important than the object of focus itself. The act of observing is more significant than the thing being observed.

Meditation instructors often start students with focusing rather than awareness to avoid confusion. If a student is simply told to sit and be aware of their breath, they may have many questions, such as "What does being aware of the breath mean? How can I just be aware of my breath? Where should I direct my awareness?" To avoid these questions, the instructor may suggest starting with focusing. They may ask the student to simply sit and focus, without worrying about awareness. The important thing early on in meditation is to develop the ability to sit and focus, regardless of what is being observed. Questions will inevitably arise, but it's important to recognize that these are just distractions.

You can see how starting meditation with focus and then transitioning to awareness works. At first, trying to focus intensely can lead to interference and distraction from your mind. With practice, you'll learn that it's easier to focus when you're relaxed rather than tense. The connection between relaxation and focus will become clear as you practice, and you'll realize that the more relaxed you are, the easier it is to maintain focus. This relaxed state of focusing eventually leads to awareness.

Awareness is simply relaxed focusing. In this state, you can accommodate questions and confusion, but intense focus does not allow for this. The issue with intense focus is that it creates a constant struggle between your intended focus and your thoughts. By its nature, focus can only be directed towards one object at a time. When focusing, you can either observe your breath or your thoughts, but not both simultaneously.

Focus is often accompanied by disturbance, agitation, and confusion because focus requires effort. Focus involves making an effort to keep only one object in your consciousness. For example, if you were told to sit and focus on an apple on a tree, it may seem simple, but you would experience significant disturbance. The more you try to intensely focus on the apple, the more agitated and disturbed your mind becomes. While trying to focus, you may hear your mind constantly distracting you with thoughts such as "Are you focusing correctly? You're getting distracted. You should relax more." This is a common experience during meditation when you are trying to focus on your breath. The easiest way to overcome this disturbance in meditation is to transition gently from focus to awareness.

Awareness is a subtle and delicate state of mind that allows you to hold multiple things in your consciousness at once. However, when you focus on something, you need to create a boundary and keep all other distractions outside of that boundary. This can be challenging because thoughts tend to wander and compete for your attention. Even if you set a boundary, thoughts will still try to push their way in, requiring effort to keep them out. For example, if you are asked to focus on a table, your mind will naturally set a boundary around it and try to ignore other distractions. However, it takes effort to keep the focus on the table and not let your mind wander.

Initially, you must begin your meditation with focus, but with enough practice, you'll learn how to simply be aware. With time, you'll find that it takes less effort to focus on your breath and that it's easier to observe it when you're relaxed and not trying too hard.

Your awareness will allow you to recognize distracting thoughts, acknowledge them, and let them go without fighting them. For example, if a thought enters your mind saying "Let's go for a walk," you can calmly respond with "No, let's sit and watch the breath." Since you're not intensely focusing on the breath, your awareness will allow you to observe both the breath and the thoughts simultaneously.

Sometimes it's impossible to completely avoid a thought, but with awareness, you can observe your breath and acknowledge the thoughts in your mind without being overly affected by them. The purpose of meditation is to stay present in the moment and avoid drifting into thoughts. If you start to drift into thoughts, you risk falling asleep instead of meditating.

The mind struggles to understand meditation and may view it as a waste of time. It is constantly pushing us to take action. When we sit still in meditation, the mind becomes restless due to its deep-seated conditioning to always be in motion. The stillness of meditation challenges the very nature of the mind, causing it to become restless. The mind dislikes monotony and sees itself as the chief source of entertainment in our lives. If it feels that it's not being entertained, it believes it's failing in its duties. This is why the monotony of meditation, such as focusing on the breath, can make us feel sleepy. The mind loves sleep because it allows it to dream without interruption. Sleep is the mind's favorite form of entertainment.

Meditation is the art of being fully awake and alert in the face of boredom. It is a valuable skill to learn. If you can learn to embrace and appreciate boredom, you can handle any challenges that life presents. Meditation is not about doing or creating something; it's about learning how to stay present in the moment and not get lost in thoughts. Being lost in thoughts is a normal part of life, and it can be entertaining. It's like watching a movie where you are the leading character, which is naturally enjoyable. Why wouldn't you like watching a movie where you are the leading character, loved and admired by all? You could do it all day!

Can you describe your meditation practice of focusing on the spine?

After years of practice, I realized that I was constantly shifting my focus within my body, trying to be aware. At times, I was focused on the inner silence, and at other times, I was observing my thoughts. I started with focusing on my breath and eventually began to observe everything happening within me - body sensations, pain and discomfort, temperature changes, emotional fluctuations, and anything else I could notice. At some point during my meditation, I realized that the tension in my spine is easy to observe, as it's always present.

Your spine is the most tense part of your body and is under more stress than any other part of your body. It takes a little awareness to recognize this. Your spine may be in pain, but you may not be aware of it because you have become accustomed to this constant discomfort. Throughout the day, there is a lot of pressure and strain on your spine, but we often ignore it. This is because we are not aware of what it feels like to not be in this constant state of physical stress on the spine.

The only time the spine is fully relaxed is when we are asleep. During the day, we have the choice to use and rest different parts of our body, such as our hands or legs, but with our spine, we do not have this choice. As long as we are awake, we are using our spine and it is under constant stress. The day I became aware of this, I started paying close attention to my spine. My spine became a central focus in my meditation practice.

There is something transformative that happens when you focus on pain during meditation. Rather than avoiding it, by intensely observing it, the experience of pain can disappear. This may seem difficult to believe, as we are used to trying to distract ourselves from pain. However, in meditation, by directing your attention towards the pain and observing it, the energy of observation can alter the way you experience pain. Although the physical source of the pain is in the body, it is the mind that makes it real. By gaining control over your mind, you can also gain control over physical sensations, including pain.

By continually observing the pain in the spine, there came a moment when I redirected my entire focus from the pain to the observer. As you continuously observe the pain in the body, you eventually become the observer. This transition from the experiencer to the observer is known as awakening.

Awakening is a moment when you become the observer. It takes consistent practice to reach this state. The body is always in a state of disturbance. In fact, when the body is completely relaxed, you tend to forget about it. Awakening is a moment when the body is completely relaxed and the mind is fully alert.

Meditation requires a balance between relaxation and alertness. If you focus solely on relaxation, your mind may become too relaxed and lead to sleepiness. The level of relaxation in the body and the level of alertness in the mind are inversely related. The more you relax your body, the more alert your mind should be in order to avoid falling asleep. This can be especially challenging when meditating in a lying down position, as the relaxed state of the body can make you feel drowsy. On the other hand, meditating in an upright position creates some tension in the body, which helps keep you awake. As you progress in your practice, you can gradually relax your body, but you must maintain a heightened level of alertness to stay awake and present.

Meditation involves a delicate balance between focus and awareness. When you focus on your breath, your mind may start to wander, and at that point, it's important to maintain your focus. Alternatively, if you find yourself getting agitated from focusing too much, it's essential to take a step back and shift to being aware. The key to successful meditation is learning when to focus and when to be aware, like a graceful dance.

MIND, BODY, AND SELF

"I have a mind, body, and spirit. Unfortunately, they're all in a complicated love triangle."

Anonymous

You have spoken about the mind, the body, and the Self. When we are meditating, we are trying to quieten the mind by observing our thoughts, though I catch myself arguing, "Go away. Go away thought." Who is arguing with the thought, and what exactly is the Self?

During meditation, the goal is to transcend or quiet the constant noise and distractions in the mind. You have to acknowledge the presence of these thoughts and distractions. Once you have recognized them, you can set the intention to become calm or release the distraction. However, you may wonder, "If all thoughts and distractions are created by the mind, then who is trying to quiet the mind?" The true self is pure consciousness and doesn't use language, but during meditation, it's common to use language to direct the mind. Although it may seem like the self is using language, it's actually an illusion because the real self isn't engaged in the conversation. The attachment to thoughts and the belief that they are one's own can lead to confusion and can hinder the meditation process.

Our true Self communicates its desire for us to awaken through the mind and thoughts. However, the mind is often cluttered with noise and distractions that can make it difficult to hear this message. The goal of meditation is to quiet the mind and transcend all forms of suffering, whether it's mental, physical, or emotional. Even if we don't consider ourselves spiritual or don't meditate, we all have an innate desire to overcome pain and suffering.

The desire to go beyond suffering is a fundamental aspect of the human experience. Some people may turn to drugs, alcohol, or extreme sports to escape their suffering, as they seek an adrenaline rush. But ultimately, the journey of life is about transcending suffering in some way or another. Every day, we face the challenge of moving beyond suffering, and we take various actions to alleviate it. For instance, if it's too hot, we might buy an air conditioner or if it's inconvenient to walk, we might buy a car. However, these solutions are temporary and require ongoing maintenance.

The Self has an inherent drive to overcome suffering, both internal and external. As we continue to listen to the mind, we gradually become aware that suffering is a never-ending cycle. This realization motivates the Self to use language to quiet the mind because it recognizes that the mind is the source of disturbance. When we tell ourselves, "I want to calm my mind, it's causing me disturbance," we are expressing the desire to overcome internal suffering. However, merely repeating this thought adds more clutter to the mind, which goes against the goal of quieting the mind.

The path to stillness lies in observing thoughts and freeing ourselves from their hold. By continually observing thoughts, their grip on us weakens, enabling us to move closer to our true essence. The depths of our being are full of peace and joy, whereas all disturbances exist only on the surface of the mind. With consistent practice, we can gradually detach ourselves from the constant grip of our thoughts and experience the peace and bliss within.

Intellectually, you may ask questions like "What is a thought?" or "How can I quiet my mind?" However, the most effective approach to quieting the mind is to regularly practice observing your thoughts. By actively making an effort to watch your thoughts, you move closer to experiencing internal peace and silence.

The Self speaks the language of stillness and silence, while the mind speaks the language of noise. The Self has no need for communication as it exists separate from the processes of life. Though you may believe that your Self is attached to your body, this attachment is merely a creation of the mind. As you delve deeper into meditation, you will come to understand that all of your attachments are simply figments of your imagination.

The Self is not attached to the body and mind. It is like the ocean and the waves - the ocean does not need the waves to exist, but the waves cannot exist without the ocean. Your body and mind are dependent on the conscious Self, but the Self does not require any support from them. The Self is eternal, conscious, and blissful, and is referred to in Sanskrit as "Satchidananda," meaning "Truth, Consciousness, and Bliss." The Self uses the body and mind as tools to express life, like paint brushes creating an artistic masterpiece.

Language is an essential tool for uncovering the truth about the Self. To truly transcend the limitations of the mind, it is important to use language wisely, rather than becoming entangled in it. Unfortunately, some individuals have turned the spiritual journey into an intellectual exercise, repeating spiritual phrases and concepts without actually applying them to their lives. Simply stating "I am not the body, I am not the mind, I am neither this nor that" without taking any action will not bring about any meaningful change. Instead of using language as a means of exploring the true nature of existence, some individuals have simply replaced their uncertainties with words, without truly understanding their meaning.

We should be mindful of using language as a mere substitute for actual experience. Words can never replace real experience. For instance, if you are feeling thirsty, you need to drink water to quench it, simply repeating the word "water" will not do the job. The same goes for the mind. If you try to relax it by repeatedly saying, "I want to relax, I want to be quiet," it will not work, it will only heighten your desire for stillness. Instead of adding more words, observe your thoughts.

You can use your intellect and awareness to differentiate between what is truly you and what is not. Be honest and discerning. Recognize when a thought arises, and do not automatically assume that it is originating from you. Rather, it is just your mind speaking. The goal of meditation is to identify the part of you that is separate from all of this, the part that is simply observing everything in a peaceful and detached manner.

One day in your meditation, you will come to realize that you can continue to listen to the constant chatter of your mind, while at the same time, remaining unaffected by it. The goal of meditation is not to eliminate your thoughts, but to learn how to coexist with them, without being consumed by them. It is to acknowledge the presence of thoughts and still maintain a sense of detachment from them.

The Self is already in a state of perfection, separate from the mind and its constant chatter. The mind is just a collection of thoughts, while the Self is a transcendent phenomenon of existence. We often confuse the mind with the Self, but the center of all living things is the Self, which is always free and complete.

The objective of meditation is to move from the periphery of the mind and reconnect with the center, the Self. This allows us to see through the illusion of separation and understand that the same life that illuminates everything else, also illuminates us. However, this can only be achieved by observing and becoming aware of the mind and its thoughts, instead of being entangled by them.

Listen to the mind, engage in conversations with it, but don't allow it to control you. Cultivate the ability to recognize that you are engaging with your mind, and stay constantly aware of your presence, your body, and the present moment. The state of being, rather than becoming, is what you are missing in life. Currently, you are overly focused on becoming something - whether it be enlightened, successful, or something else. But there is nothing to become, because you are already complete just as you are. The key is to realize and understand this truth.

To embark on the journey of discovering your authentic Self, it's essential to differentiate yourself from everything that is not you. This involves having a clear intellectual understanding that you are not just the mind or the body. In the early stages of my meditation practice, I realized this through a process of intellectual inquiry, which led me to further explore this idea. I spent a lot of time reading and questioning, and eventually came to the conclusion that I was separate from both the mind and the body. This realization became so vivid that I couldn't ignore it, and it drove me to deepen my meditation practice.

Since I didn't have a teacher to guide me, I had to rely on my own questioning and self-reflection to come to this understanding. It was through this introspective process that I was able to uncover the truth about my authentic Self, and it was a discovery that I could not turn back from.

In order to truly understand that you are not just your mind or body, it is necessary to engage in your own inner inquiry, rather than simply relying on a teacher's theoretical understanding. A teacher can offer guidance, but without personal exploration, you may find yourself constantly searching for a better teacher.

To deepen your meditation practice, it is crucial to shift your focus inward and have your own personal experiences.

Although you may intellectually believe that you are more than just your mind and body, it is still just an assumption until you experience it for yourself. To make progress in meditation, you have to adopt this assumption and examine everything as if you are separate from your mind and body. This shift in perspective can alter the way you view yourself and others, changing your experience of life. By taking a closer look at your assumption that you are only the sum of your thoughts and physical actions, you can discover a deeper aspect of yourself that provides stability and peace in the midst of life's chaos.

The Sanskrit term "Viveka" means the ability to distinguish between truth and untruth. By utilizing this power of discrimination, you can separate yourself from all that you are not. You can sharpen your intellect like a tool and use it to examine your experiences in life. With a sharp intellect, you can cut through many limitations and come closer to realizing your true self. "Viveka" can help you differentiate between what you are and what you are not, leading you to the essential question, "If I am not my mind or body, then what am I?" This inquiry can lead you deeper into meditation.

While intellectual inquiry alone cannot lead you to a direct realization of the Truth, it can assist you in eliminating what you are not. By utilizing the power of discrimination, you can logically deduce that there is something more to you beyond your mind and body. For instance, you can observe your hand closely for a month and see that it is distinct from your true Self. Even if your hand were to be gone, you would still feel complete. This critical observation and analysis can be applied to understanding the distinction between your mind and body and your true Self. By sharpening your intellect, you can separate yourself from your mind and body and come closer to realizing your true nature.

Let's examine another example to understand the idea better. When you drink a cup of tea, you experience its warmth, taste, smell, and pleasure. But are these experiences happening to you or to your body? Is it you who has an interest in the tea, or is it your body? By using your power of discrimination, you can clearly see that drinking a cup of tea is solely an experience of the body; you are merely the observer of this process. How can you be sure of this? For example, if the tea is too hot, would you still enjoy it in the same way? Of course not, because it would burn your mouth, and your body would immediately reject it. The entire experience of drinking tea is a conditioned experience of the body. The body has become accustomed to liking tea in a certain way and craves the experience. If there was no separation between you and your body, why would there be a constant conflict between your desires and your body's desires? This conflict itself should indicate to you that you are something other than your body.

A sharp sense of observation will aid you in staying present and observing your mind and body. This practice, in and of itself, will gradually deepen your comprehension of life. It may seem inconsequential at first, but as you get into the habit of observing your mind and body, the experience can be both enlightening and entertaining. Intellectually, what you aim to understand is the nature of the mind and body, and their relationship to each other. This is not enlightenment, but it is a step towards it. Once you grasp this, you can embark on the journey to discover who you truly are. When you intellectually understand that you are not just the mind or body, it is only a matter of time before you experience this for yourself. Your intellectual understanding will eventually aid you in distinguishing the experiences of your mind, body, and Self, and the clarity that arises from this distinction will leave you astounded.

CLINGING TO WORDS

"Silence is the language of God, all else is poor translation."

Rumi

Every morning I see the chickens wandering around, and when they look at a leaf, they look at it as if they have never seen it before. Why can't I look at the same leaf with that much curiosity?

What you are really asking is, 'Why do we hold onto things, ideas, concepts, places, or people?' You observed the chickens and noted that they remain as curious as they were when they were born, still examining each leaf as if it were new to them. However, when you look at a leaf, you have already made the assumption that you know it's a leaf, so it lacks excitement for you.

We exhibit this same behavior towards everything. We come across something new and are intrigued for a short period, only to eventually lose interest. For animals, each day brings new experiences and is a fresh start. Boredom arises from language: humans use language, while animals do not. This simple difference plays a critical role in shaping our experiences. When a chicken looks at a leaf, it does not have a concept of what it is seeing because it does not have a word for "leaf." Without a label, every leaf is a unique and novel experience. However, for you, having a name for a leaf means you believe you have a complete understanding of all leaves.

Boredom sets in when our focus shifts from the physical leaf to the label we have assigned to it, as we have given a single name to all leaves. If we observe ten different leaves, our mind may tell us, 'You're looking at a leaf again, you're seeing the same thing.' However, in reality, no two leaves are exactly alike. The word "leaf" is just a convenient label we use to categorize objects that have similar appearances. This can restrict our perception and lead to attachment to our knowledge. It is this attachment to the knowledge of something that causes boredom. When we abandon language and perceive things as they truly are, we cannot cling to them, and boredom becomes impossible.

The little boy meandered into the room where his mother was sitting at her desk writing. She glanced down at him and saw that he was carrying a precious vase that her grandmother had given her. Almost absentmindedly she said to him, "Robert, go put the vase down before you drop it and break it." "I can't," he replied, "I can't get my hand out."

"Of course you can," she said, "you got it down there." He said, "I know mom, but it won't come out." The neck of the vase was very narrow and his hand had fit neatly inside and it was now up to his wrist. He continued to insist that he could not get it out. Growing a little concerned, his mother called out to his dad.

Dad calmly took control and began gently pulling the arm trying to extract the hand from the vase. He tried loosening it up with soapy water. Still nothing. He then got some vegetable oil from the kitchen and poured it around the wrist and let it seep into the vase. He wiggled it some. It still did not budge.

"I give up," the dad said in desperation. "I'd give a dollar right now to know how to get it out."

"Really?" little Robert exclaimed. Then they heard a clinking sound and his hand slid right out of the vase. They turned the vase upside down and a penny plopped out. "What's this?" they said in unison.

"Oh, that's the penny I put inside. I wanted to get it out so I was clutching it in my hand. But when I heard Dad say he would give a dollar to have the vase free, I let go."

Every experience in existence occurs exactly as it should, and our minds are an integral part of this process. When we use language, we claim ownership of that experience. When we look at a leaf, it simply exists, and we do not possess it. The moment we say it is a leaf, we claim ownership of it, as at that moment, we have a greater understanding of it than any other creature.

To all other creatures, a leaf remains a mystery. For us, however, a leaf is no longer a mystery as we have a definition for it: 'A leaf performs photosynthesis, is usually green, comes in various shapes, and eventually withers and dies.' Once we attach this label to a leaf, our mind tells us, 'You already know what a leaf is, why bother being curious about another one?' In this way, our mind prevents us from seeing each leaf as if it were brand new.

Imagine if we didn't have language. Without the knowledge that this is a table, every time we looked at it, we would see something new, as it is not simply a table. When we gaze upon this wooden table, we are essentially looking at a frozen moment in time, aren't we? This table holds the memories of everything that happened during its existence. Every scratch and imperfection is a memory, but our mind tells us, 'You're crazy, that's just a table.' We listen to our mind and do not seek out new discoveries. Similarly, we categorize the world with labels, and the moment we do so, the moment we use language, we diminish the beauty of whatever it is we are labeling.

This is where the challenge lies: To fully appreciate and relish life, we must embrace our inner child and revisit the innocent part of our mind. We must go back to a time when we didn't have access to language, when we didn't know that the world was full of things. When we let go of language, we become more attentive.

It is language that causes us to delve deeper into boredom. Of course, without language, we would not be able to distinguish between different objects and experiences, but most of the time, we don't need language to enjoy life. We can experience the beauty of life without words, especially if we refrain from using any.

Try this: the next time you look at a rose, do so without thinking of the word "rose," without labeling it as a rose. Observe how the silence enhances the beauty of the rose. We get bored easily because we live in a world of words created by our mind. When we step away from this mental chatter and enter the stillness of life, we will see how truly beautiful existence is.

Language presents a significant obstacle to achieving inner stillness, yet without it, we would not know what to surpass. Language is an important aspect of life and it is essential that we comprehend its purpose, how to use it, when to use it, and when to let go of it.

If we do not fully understand language, our mind will cling to it blindly. The mind cannot value new experiences if it clings to language.

Throughout the day, pay attention to your inner dialogue. Then, for a brief period, quiet your mind completely: look at something without labeling it, enjoy a cup of tea without thinking about it, savor a delicious meal without verbalizing it. You will notice that 'not talking about it' means more than simply not speaking out loud. You should also refrain from describing the experience in your thoughts. When you do not narrate your experience, it remains pure and genuine. The experience of life is greatly enriched when you stop talking about it. In this sense, boredom does not exist in reality. Boredom is simply a repetitive voice in your head.

Without language, all life experiences become simple, unencumbered experiences. They never cling to us. They become nothing more than pure, fleeting moments. We use language to recall an experience, to categorize and manipulate it, and it becomes a part of our memory. We constantly compare new experiences to past ones, which prevents us from seeing people and things as though for the first time.

Imagine the pure joy of waking up each morning with no prior knowledge of the day. How would it feel to encounter someone for the first time without knowing their name or anything about them? Our eyes would be wide open with curiosity, eager to learn more about them. However, now, when we look at someone, our mind immediately starts its labeling process.

Imagine a world where you have not been introduced to language. Imagine not knowing what language is, not being able to name things, and not even being aware of your own name. To say, 'I exist,' you need language. Without language, you would still exist, still walk, eat, and breathe, but there would be no observer to witness these processes and no one to question your actions. There would be no one to stand in front of a mirror and say, 'I look like this,' as language is necessary for these experiences.

Our world is merely a collection of individual experiences held together by language. Language acts as the adhesive that unifies everything. When we let go of language, the entire universe becomes a subjective, personal experience. Without language, there is no division between us and what we are experiencing. Existence is not a static physical space that we simply occupy. It is far more enigmatic than we can imagine. The greatest enigma of all is, of course, the enigma of ourselves.

Reality is only what we can perceive in the present moment. Everything beyond this moment belongs to the imaginary world of the mind. Our world is simply the way we have imagined it to be. I'm not denying that there is an objective world out there, but it is not your world. Your world is simply a collection of your experiences. It cannot be anything more than what you have experienced and cannot exist in any other form independent of the language you use to describe it.

Your world is simply your story. You have used language to construct your entire world. If you didn't have the word 'world,' you wouldn't even know it existed. Imagine if you were living in a jungle, completely isolated from the rest of the world. What would your world be? Your world would just be a collection of your experiences. We often forget that it is language that gives meaning to words like 'world,' 'universe,' 'space,' and 'time.' These are just words. If you remove the word 'time,' where is 'time'? Show it to me, put it in a bottle and give it to me, let's see!

Our language and the stories we craft with it contribute to our sense of boredom. We tend to feel bored when we perceive the same things happening repeatedly in our lives. Our story, which is essentially our entire life, can create this pattern of monotony. We crave new experiences, and every moment in existence is new. However, our language can restrict our perception and trap us in a set pattern of seeing things. While each day is fresh and new, we often fail to appreciate this and instead see each day as being the same with only minor variations. Boredom is a human problem and is one of the saddest feelings we can experience. Even though existence greets us with fresh beauty, joy, and wonders every morning, we still feel bored. Ultimately, boredom is a result of our language and our perception, and has nothing to do with existence itself.

The use of language can trap us in our own perceptions of reality. When we use language to describe an experience, we limit ourselves to that description and hold onto it. The key to being present is to immerse yourself fully in the experience, without labeling or narrating it in your mind. For instance, when observing your breath, don't think about the fact that you're observing your breath; simply engage in the experience. By looking at something as if it were the first time, you allow yourself to experience it fully without the limitations of language.

Our minds have a tendency to narrate every experience, even when it's not necessary. It is only when we recognize that our minds do not enhance the quality of our lives, but rather limit us to our perceptions, that we can seek something deeper. Language serves as a guide to remind us of our search, but we should not become attached to it and forget our ultimate destination. By letting go of language and allowing ourselves to fully engage in the present moment, we can experience the beauty of existence without limitation.

MEDITATION SHOULD BE DISTURBING

"The more regularly and the more deeply you meditate, the sooner you will find yourself acting always from a center of peace."

J. Donald Walters

How do I deal with disturbances during meditation?

The journey towards self-improvement is full of effort and obstacles. If you find yourself without any effort or challenges, it is a sign that you are not making progress. There is no growth without effort. To excel in anything, you must put in the necessary time and effort through practice.

For example, if you want to become proficient in a sport, would you seek opportunities to relax and take it easy, or would you look for challenges and obstacles to overcome? Would you play against easy opponents, or would you prefer to face tough and experienced players? In sports, even a slight advantage over your opponent can lead to victory. In this sense, it is your opponents who determine your skill level and progress more than anything else.

This concept applies to many aspects of life. Your struggles, obstacles, opponents, and challenges shape you as a person and help you grow. This is also true in meditation, where growth occurs through facing and overcoming disturbances.

Meditation presents you with the ultimate challenge, as the obstacles you face are not external, but internal. Your own mind and body are the greatest hindrances in meditation. The entire process of meditation involves overcoming the constant distractions and agitation of the mind and body.

The mind and body are not naturally inclined to relaxation and stillness. They have been conditioned to action, effort, and agitation. When you embark on the journey of self-improvement through meditation, this conditioning of the mind and body becomes the biggest challenge. As a result, meditation requires a great deal of effort. It involves a deliberate attempt to go beyond the constant distractions of the mind and body, to reach a state of inner peace and stillness.

As practitioners, we should not focus on seeking relaxation during meditation. Relaxation should be a natural byproduct of a deepening meditation practice. If our primary goal is relaxation, we may be disappointed. Instead, we should embrace the challenges and distractions that arise during meditation.

Initially, meditation should be challenging. The process of trying to keep the mind and body still at the same time requires a great deal of effort and may cause significant disturbance. There will be moments when meditation will be effortless and relaxing, and other times when it will be extremely difficult. You will find that meditating at night is particularly challenging because it is difficult to stay awake. However, you should make a conscious effort to meditate at night because it presents a great challenge to overcome.

Meditation is about embracing the disturbance and working through it, not about escaping from it. It requires effort and determination to go deeper and achieve a state of inner peace and stillness. The goal of meditation is to quiet the mind without losing awareness and to relax the body without being disturbed. When both of these elements are present in your meditation, you can feel satisfied. Disturbances during meditation provide opportunities for growth and self-reflection.

In the beginning, it is not necessary to focus solely on relaxation. Instead, we should focus on gaining a deeper understanding. Relaxation in meditation is a natural result of increased understanding of the mind and body. Disturbances offer opportunities to gain insight into the nature of the mind and body.

To transcend the limitations of the mind and body, it is necessary to understand their nature. The nature of the mind is sleep, and the nature of the body is disturbance. By embracing and working through these disturbances, we can deepen our understanding of the mind and body and eventually achieve a state of relaxation and stillness in meditation.

The mind often resists staying present with the body, as it is naturally inclined to wander and explore. If left unchecked, the mind can easily become lost in thoughts. If relaxed too much, it will go to sleep. Similarly, the nature of the body is disturbance, and if we sit for too long, it will want to get up and move. If we move for too long, it will want to rest. The body also requires continuous care and nourishment which adds to the distraction. These constant disturbances are what we aim to overcome in meditation.

As long as there are disturbances and a tendency to sleep, there is still work to be done in meditation. If you seek deeper understanding, relaxation should not be your primary focus. Instead, you must focus on the disturbances within, so that you can eventually transcend them.

A seeker is a unique individual who is searching for experiences that many people try to avoid. They seek out pain in order to understand and transcend it. However, it is important to distinguish between a seeker and a person who is acting irrationally. A seeker is attempting to comprehend the nature of pain, while a person who is acting irrationally is willingly causing pain to themselves for no reason.

Pain is an important aspect of the meditation journey. It serves as a reminder that there is always room for growth and improvement. As the poet Rumi said, "Wound is the door through which light enters." Pain can serve as a door to inner understanding and bliss. As a seeker, you should not try to escape or intentionally cause pain. Instead, you should embrace it and use it as a tool for growth and self-reflection. Emotional pain, psychological pain, and physical pain can all lead to deeper understanding and a state of inner peace.

It's essential to understand that even though meditation can sometimes feel pleasant and easy, this does not always signify that you're progressing on a deeper level. To truly advance your meditation practice, you must face the obstacles and disruptions that may arise, such as pain or distractions. While these moments may seem challenging, they are precisely the times when your meditation practice is deepening. By persisting through these difficulties, you'll have the chance to develop and improve your skills. However, it's also crucial to recognize the importance of savoring the times when meditation feels effortless and enjoyable. Remember, the ultimate goal of meditation is self-realization, and working through these challenges is a necessary part of the journey towards achieving that goal.

BEYOND HAPPINESS

"I think and think and think, I've thought myself out of happiness one million times, but never once into it."

Jonathan Safran Foer

Is happiness the ultimate goal of life?

Happiness is closely linked to the nature of the mind. The mind is constantly oscillating between the past and future, while happiness is experienced in the present moment. It is through these fluctuations in the mind that we can experience moments of happiness. For example, let's say you wake up to find a cup of coffee on the table. After taking a sip, you realize it's not as hot as you prefer. This experience triggers a response in you, and you express your dissatisfaction. The following day, you approach your coffee with the expectation that it might not be hot enough, but this time it's at the perfect temperature, and you feel a moment of happiness.

In this example, the experience of happiness is not located in the physical objects of the coffee, the mouth, or the cup. Rather, happiness arises from our own expectations. Happiness is just another aspect of expectation. When we hold certain expectations and they are fulfilled, we experience happiness.

Conversely, if our expectations are not met, we experience unhappiness. This pattern is repeated throughout our daily lives, where we unconsciously form expectations based on previous experiences. Therefore, happiness is not an independent entity that exists in itself, but is a mental phenomenon that arises from the alignment of events with our expectations. We should not consider happiness as the ultimate goal of human life.

It's important to recognize that pain and suffering are an inevitable part of life, just as happiness is. The nature of happiness is fleeting and temporary, and it's impossible to be happy all the time. Our society has placed an overemphasis on the pursuit of happiness as the ultimate goal of life. However, this mindset can actually contribute to our unhappiness. We have been conditioned to believe that happiness is the solution to all of our problems, and we spend our lives chasing after it, only to find that it is not a sustainable state of being. It's essential to acknowledge the impermanence of happiness and the inevitability of suffering, and learn to find contentment in the present moment, regardless of whether we are experiencing happiness or not.

As humans, we need a balance of happiness and misery in our lives. Rejecting misery and pursuing happiness exclusively will create an unbalanced life. Striving to be happy all the time can be counterproductive and lead to unhappiness. There are moments in life when we experience pain, suffering, and sadness, and these emotions are necessary for our growth and development. Rejecting these emotions and solely seeking happiness can lead to inner conflict and further suffering.

Living in the present moment means accepting and embracing all emotions and experiences without preference or aversion. Both happiness and sadness are integral parts of life, and the key is to approach them with equanimity. When happiness arises, fully immerse yourself in the joy and appreciate the moment. Similarly, when pain and suffering arise, allow yourself to feel them without resistance. By accepting all emotions equally, we can experience life in all its complexity and richness.

The pursuit of happiness should not be the ultimate goal of life, as it can lead to an unbalanced and unrealistic expectation. Instead, we are searching for a sense of certainty and fulfillment that transcends both pleasure and pain. This is why people are driven to climb mountains or participate in extreme sports, because they offer a moment of transcendence beyond our everyday experiences. Unfortunately, some individuals turn to addictive substances like drugs and alcohol, seeking a temporary feeling of bliss to escape from their difficulties.

As human beings, our ultimate pursuit is to find a sense of inner bliss and certainty. This sense of complete freedom transcends the limitations of our minds and bodies, allowing us to experience ourselves fully. However, we often resort to indirect means like drugs, alcohol, and sex to experience fleeting moments of this bliss. In truth, the direct path to lasting bliss is through spirituality and meditation. By embarking on a journey of self-discovery, we can find our true selves and attain the lasting inner bliss that we seek.

The journey of self-discovery involves much more than just fleeting moments of happiness. It is the quest to unravel the mystery of who we truly are, which makes life both challenging and fulfilling. Every experience we encounter in life is an opportunity to gain insight and clarity about this mystery. However, it is the uncertainty of this quest that makes it the greatest challenge. Moments of unhappiness can be difficult, but it is the moments of not knowing that are truly overwhelming. Our lives are spent in a constant search for answers about our true selves, and this search can often feel like a prison of ignorance. The only time we experience true freedom is in moments of bliss when we transcend the limitations of our minds and bodies. In all other moments, we are bound by our thoughts and physical forms.

Bliss and certainty are not something we can find externally; they exist within us. The external world is simply a reflection of the uncertainty we carry inside. Seeking these qualities outside of ourselves is futile, as we will never find a perfect example of bliss and certainty in the external world. The path to discovering these qualities lies within, through the practice of meditation. Meditation allows us to transcend the limitations of the mind and body, experiencing a moment of pure internal bliss and certainty. This is why external achievements cannot provide lasting happiness or certainty, as we can still feel unhappy and uncertain on the inside. The search for certainty outside of ourselves only leads to more pain and suffering, as we continue to pursue happiness, which is merely a disguise for uncertainty. To find true bliss and certainty, we must look beyond fleeting moments of happiness and turn inward.

WHY SEARCH FOR AWAKENING?

"Be a light to yourself. You are enough to yourself."

Buddha

You said that our 'Self' is something eternal, something that never dies. Why should I spend so much time and energy to become Enlightened if I am eternal anyway? If I am going to come back again and again in different bodies, in different lifetimes, what's the necessity of becoming Enlightened?

You need to recognize that your mind is creating these questions as obstacles on your journey towards self-realization. The mind can be resistant to the hard work and challenges that come with meditation, and so it may ask, "What is the purpose? Why should I bother?" as a means of avoiding the effort.

Even if you experience constant happiness and bliss, there is still an inner longing to understand the deeper purpose of life. This longing is reflected in your constant search for pleasure, meaning, and connection. The pursuit of spiritual enlightenment is not a matter of choice, but rather an innate desire within us. To ignore this desire is to miss the whole point of living.

To experience awakening is the ultimate goal for anyone seeking true and profound experiences. To deny this experience is to deny yourself any true experience. Other experiences in life may be like taking small sips, but awakening is like quenching your thirst with a full glass of water. You may be searching for answers to life's questions and yearning for a deeper understanding of yourself and the world around you. The ultimate experience that can satisfy this thirst is spiritual awakening.

Without even realizing it, we are constantly searching for the bliss of awakening in every aspect of our lives. This is why material objects and external experiences can never truly satisfy us. We may attain some level of contentment when we achieve our goals or find love, but this satisfaction is fleeting and ultimately unfulfilling. We continue to search for new experiences, hoping that they will provide us with lasting happiness.

We believe that success, love, and fame will bring us satisfaction and fulfillment. However, we rarely examine the deeper motivations behind our desires. At the heart of all our desires is a fundamental need for the internal bliss that can only be attained through spiritual awakening. If we ignore this need and focus solely on external experiences, we condemn ourselves to a life of unfulfilled desires and a constant search for something more.

In our daily lives, we are constantly seeking for something more than what we currently have. We may wonder why we feel unfulfilled, why we are constantly searching for something better. These questions are actually expressions of our true spiritual desire for awakening and enlightenment, which can sometimes become disguised by the materialistic language of the world. It's important to recognize that our thirst for spiritual awakening is genuine and should not be dismissed as a mere coincidence or something that we are told to pursue. Instead, we should embrace this desire and strive for awakening because it is what we truly crave deep down inside.

The language of spiritual awakening is not commonly used in our daily lives because we are not often surrounded by enlightened individuals who can guide us towards it. Instead, we often find ourselves surrounded by people with their own agendas, and we pursue desires not for our own happiness, but to please others. It's worth taking a moment to reflect on how much time we spend each day pursuing our own happiness versus trying to make others happy. Although we may ignore our innate desire for awakening for a while, we must eventually come to realize that what we seek is not external, but within ourselves.

> Creation said: "I want to hide something from the humans until they are ready for it. It is the realization that they create their own reality."
> The eagle said, "Give it to me. I will take it to the moon."
> The Creator said, "No, one day they will go there and find it."
> The salmon said, "I will bury it on the bottom of the ocean."

The Creator said, "No, they will go there, too."

The buffalo said, "I will bury it on the Great Plains."

The Creator said, "They will cut into the skin of the earth and find it even there."

Grandmother, who lives in the breast of Mother Earth, and who has no physical eyes but sees with spiritual eyes, said, "Put it inside of them."

And the Creator said, "It is done."

In a world that glorifies excess and consumerism, the spiritual quest for answers to life's fundamental questions can seem unremarkable and unassuming. Our culture is steeped in skepticism, and it can be difficult to embrace spiritual practices and ideas that are often misunderstood or dismissed. This lack of acceptance makes the path to self-discovery through meditation and spirituality an uphill battle, not because meditation is inherently difficult, but because we lack the supportive societal structures that make such endeavors easier. To embark on this path, individuals must free themselves from the shackles of social conditioning and be willing to pursue their authentic selves.

The journey towards spiritual discovery is one that we all embark on, whether we are aware of it or not. It starts with the moment we become conscious of our individuality and start questioning our existence. The seed of self-discovery is planted, and it cannot be destroyed. Each of us may have a different path and timeline, with some seeds germinating quicker than others. However, we will all eventually reach our destination, be it in this lifetime or the next. The realization that we are already on the path is the first step towards spiritual growth.

When Buddha was teaching, he encountered people who would ask him philosophical questions in hopes of finding a shortcut to spiritual enlightenment. Buddha recognized that these questions were often a way to avoid putting in the necessary effort to meditate and attain self-realization. Instead of providing answers to their questions, Buddha would direct their attention to the fundamental truth. He would ask if they acknowledged that there was suffering in their lives. If they answered yes, he would encourage them to go beyond that suffering and follow the path he offered. The path would take them beyond suffering, and the further they traveled on the path, the less suffering they would experience.

The journey towards self-realization is not an overnight process; it is a gradual and continuous path. The more we meditate and delve deeper into our spiritual practices, the more we can alleviate our pain and suffering. Pain is an unavoidable part of the human experience, whether it is emotional, psychological, physical, or existential. Just because we may seem happy on the outside, it does not mean that we are at peace within. It is common to feel inner turmoil and discomfort, a yearning for something more, or a sense of disconnection in the world. As long as we experience these pains, we must continue our quest for self-realization.

The path to self-realization is not a one-time destination that one can reach, but rather an ongoing process of shedding layers of conditioning and discovering one's true inner self. The journey is not about gaining material possessions or external achievements, but about releasing the negative emotions and thought patterns that hold us back. In fact, when someone once asked Buddha what he had achieved through all his years of meditation, he responded that he had not attained anything, but instead had lost things such as anger, jealousy, fear, frustration, and worry. These losses are incredibly valuable and worthwhile, and are what make the journey of self-realization so meaningful.

The process of spiritual growth remains the same, whether you refer to it as awakening, enlightenment, realization, or becoming spiritual. It involves a conscious decision to shift your attention inward and seek answers within yourself. The first step towards this journey is to trust that there is an inner world beyond the mind and body. Without this trust, you will never make an effort to explore your inner self. It is essential to approach this journey with an open mind and avoid preconceived notions about the meaning of life, as this can close off mental pathways before even starting.

The journey towards self-realization begins with acknowledging that there is more to you than what you currently know. It takes humility and curiosity to say, "I've explored the external world, and now I want to look within." Self-realization is a process of delving deeper into yourself. As you continue on this journey, you will reach a point where your introspection will reveal your true nature. This moment of awakening is when the illusions of life and suffering fade away, and you gain an understanding of who you are, what the body and mind are, and why you were experiencing unnecessary pain.

> A man is walking home at night and sees what appears to be a snake. Immediately he is startled and scared. The next day, when there is enough light, he looks at the snake on his way out of the village and sees that it is not a snake. It was just a rope that had fallen there. When he could not see the rope clearly in darkness, he mistook it for a snake and was almost scared to death.

The fear that grips us is often based on illusions that arise from a lack of clarity or understanding. This is true even for the simplest of things, like a rope that we cannot see clearly, which can scare us. The greatest illusions that we face are rooted in our ignorance of the truth of life and death. We identify with our temporary physical bodies and fear the aging process and the passage of time. This fear distracts us from finding peace, enjoying life, and unlocking its full potential. We mistake the appearances and expressions of life for life itself, just as we may mistake a rope for a snake.

As you awaken to the truth of your being, you will realize that fear was merely a creation of the mind. The mind's projections and illusions keep us trapped in a state of fear and anxiety. Only by awakening from this state of slumber can we see through these illusions and come to understand that there is nothing to fear. Everyone experiences fear to some degree, whether it be fear of failure, aging, rejection, or death. But the solution to overcoming these fears lies in awakening to our true nature.

FROM CONCEPTS TO EXPERIENCE

"True virtue is knowing the self not by intellectual knowledge but by pure silence."

Amit Ray

How can I go beyond excessive thinking and deepen my connection to life?

The essence of meditation is to transcend from the realm of concepts to that of experience. The goal is to experience life as it is, through the pristine clarity of our consciousness, unobstructed by the filter of thoughts. Though thoughts are a valid way to perceive reality, it is just one of the many ways we can experience the world around us. We can also engage our senses to explore the world - by feeling, touching, smelling, tasting, and seeing things. Meditation empowers us to dive deeper into our consciousness and experience the world with heightened awareness, with all our senses in sync, free from the veil of thoughts.

Many of us tend to rely heavily on our sense of sight to understand and interact with the world around us. However, for people who have been blind since birth, their perception of reality is shaped by their other senses. Despite the lack of visual input, these individuals are still able to navigate the world and understand their surroundings through touch, taste, hearing, and smell. In fact, their other senses often become more heightened to compensate for the absence of vision. Blind individuals can get a clear understanding of an object through touching it and their perception of reality may differ from those who can see, but they are not necessarily missing out on anything. Their unique experiences and abilities allow them to interact with the world in a different way.

In our lives, we have given a lot of importance to our thinking and have overlooked the significance of our other senses. We often think that understanding reality is possible only through thinking, analyzing, and contemplating. When we hear a word like "tree," our mind starts to process information, generating thoughts such as what the tree looks like or what fruit it bears. However, to break free from the trap of letting our thoughts dominate and interfere with our perception, it is essential to explore and tap into our other senses. Mindfulness and meditation can be great tools to help us enhance our perception and gain a deeper understanding of the reality that surrounds us.

If you want to truly understand a tree, try not to assume anything about it. Instead, take a mindful approach by touching the tree, feeling its bark with your hands, and directing all of your attention to it. By doing so, the tree will unveil its true nature to you in a way that you may not have experienced before. Although you may have seen numerous trees throughout your life, most of them have remained silent to you. However, by consciously engaging with the tree through touch and observation, it will communicate with you and expose its essence. Connecting with things on a personal level is the only way to fully comprehend their true nature.

To reconnect with our physical selves and see the world objectively, we need to move beyond just relying on our thoughts. Although thinking can be helpful for reflection, it's not the most effective tool for gaining a genuine understanding of the world around us. Instead, we should tap into our other senses - like sight, touch, taste, smell, and hearing - to get a more complete picture of reality. The act of thinking is like trying to understand life by repeating what has already been experienced, which can sometimes cloud our perception with unnecessary information and interpretations. By stepping away from our reliance on thinking and focusing on our senses, we can gain a deeper understanding of the world and experience it in a more genuine way.

Mindfulness and meditation provide a way for us to access our senses and connect with the world around us in a more intimate and direct way. Rather than being preoccupied with our thoughts and missing out on the present moment, we can fully engage with our experiences and appreciate the world more deeply. By connecting with our inner silence, we can cultivate awareness and come back to the present moment, to experience life in its fullness. By being fully present and attentive to our senses, we can gain a more profound understanding and appreciation of the world around us.

We have become so consumed by our thoughts that we often overlook the richness and beauty of the present moment. We have convinced ourselves that the significance of life lies only in our thoughts, leading us to a monotonous existence where routine tasks like eating and showering become mindless and unremarkable. We don't fully experience these moments and instead distract ourselves with other things like watching TV or thinking about unrelated matters. Our minds are preoccupied, leaving us unaware of the richness and depth of these experiences. However, to truly appreciate life, we need to shift our focus from our thoughts and be fully present in the moment. This will allow us to rediscover the beauty and depth of everyday moments that we have overlooked.

One might ask, "Why waste time being mindful of mundane tasks, instead of thinking about something important?" The answer is simple - thinking is purely imaginary, while mindfulness is real. There is no better way to control the direction of your life than by being vigilant of what you're doing in the present moment.

The key to practicing mindfulness is to shift your focus from the experiences of the mind to the sensations of the body. Your mind is constantly occupied with thoughts, be it memories of the past or worries about the future, but you can use your body as a tool to bring your awareness to the present moment. Remind yourself to pay attention to the sensations on your skin, the rhythm of your breath, the warmth of the sun, and the wind in your hair. Open your ears to the sounds around you, whether it be the chirping of birds, the hum of insects, music, or people talking. By focusing on your bodily sensations and the sounds in your environment, you can tap into a different kind of joy and experience existence in a new and vivid way.

Being fully present in the moment is essential to experiencing life in a meaningful way. When we are lost in thought, we are not fully engaged with the present, and we miss out on the richness of life. Mindfulness allows us to be more aware of our surroundings and the present moment, which enables us to more effectively address problems and situations. When we become consumed by thoughts and are unable to break free from them, it can be incredibly distressing. Cultivating a habit of mindfulness, such as paying attention to the sensations in our body, may seem simple, but it can make a significant difference, particularly when your mind is racing and out of control.

Buddha says, "The root of all suffering is attachment." But attachment to what exactly? The answer is attachment to the mind. Our problems with the ego, emotional pain, and irrational states of mind all stem from being too attached to our minds. We don't usually question the mind, which can lead to a lot of unnecessary problems. Our bodies, on the other hand, only care about fulfilling basic needs like food, sex, and comfort. It is our minds that create all other desires. To be closer to reality, we need to be closer to the body. The further we move away from the body, the more complicated and confusing life can become.

It is essential to pay attention to the experiences of the body instead of being lost in thought. The body is a crucial aspect of our existence and is the only reality we have in this life. The mind can create abstract and imaginary ideas, but it is the body that holds the truth of who we are. It's important to ground ourselves in the physical experiences of the body instead of solely relying on our thoughts. Although thoughts can help us solve problems and understand others, they can't replace the reality of physical experiences. Unfortunately, as a society, we tend to focus more on the imagined experiences of the mind and ignore the significance of our bodies.

In modern times, our activities have shifted from being physical to being more mental in nature. Activities like dancing, painting, singing, and knitting are becoming increasingly rare. When we reflect on our childhood, we often recall a wider range of activities and hobbies that we enjoyed, but as we grow older, these interests are replaced by a singular preoccupation with thinking. Unfortunately, this shift towards excessive thinking is one of the primary reasons behind the rising levels of stress, anxiety, and worry in our society. The key to combating these problems lies in learning to live in the present moment and being mindful of the experiences of our bodies.

The mind-body imbalance is a major cause of disorder in our lives. We spend most of our time lost in our thoughts, disconnected from our bodies. This lack of balance can lead to superficial and meaningless questions that do not contribute to our well-being. The body, on the other hand, is concerned with genuine and practical concerns like how to overcome pain or find happiness. Questions about the afterlife or other abstract concepts do not interest the body. By restoring the balance between the mind and body, we can reduce the chaos in our lives and focus on what truly matters.

Listening to our body is crucial to leading a pain-free and fulfilling life. The body has its own way of communicating with us through different sensations like hunger, thirst, pain, and discomfort, and it's up to us to tune in and listen. Unlike the mind, the body never deceives us and provides clear, direct feedback. Ignoring the signals from our body can lead to an endless cycle of pain and discomfort.

To establish a strong connection with our body, we must take the time to become familiar with it and develop an appreciation for it. This means being mindful of the sensations and messages our body sends, such as hunger or fatigue, and responding appropriately. The body has its own language and by listening to it, we can better understand what it needs and how to take care of it.

Your body is not just a physical vessel, it is also the means through which you experience and perceive the world. It is only through the body that the world has any meaning to us. Through meditation, the balance between the mind and body can be restored. With consistent practice, you will become equally aware of both your mind and body, and eventually, your attention will be fully focused on your body. This heightened state of awareness and tranquility will bring immense joy and lead to a deeper understanding of the reality around us. By shifting our attention from the mind to the body, we can move from imaginary concepts to real experiences, allowing us to fully engage with and appreciate the present moment.

The mind is filled with countless ideas and concepts about life, but it doesn't offer solutions, only problems. However, the body holds the key to solving these problems. When we shift our focus from concepts to actual experiences, we gain greater control over both our mind and body. This allows us to move between the two effortlessly. Unfortunately, we often find ourselves trapped in our thoughts and don't know how to escape. But by paying attention to our body and experiencing its sensations regularly, we can find a way out. By doing so, we can transform our understanding of life from abstract concepts to a tangible reality. Your body is a gateway to bliss.

FINDING YOUR SELF

"Waking up is not a selfish pursuit of happiness, it is a revolutionary stance, from the inside out, for the benefit of all beings in existence."

Noah Levine

Sometimes I feel so alienated from life. When I reflect on my life, it feels like something is missing. What is my True Self and how can I find it?

When we think about the experience of being alive, we often only consider our own bodily sensations and experiences. We wake up in the morning and feel like we're "coming alive" as we become aware of our surroundings. But what if being alive is not just an individual phenomenon? What if aliveness is a fundamental aspect of existence itself? What if we are actually swimming in an ocean of aliveness, but we are completely unaware of it? This is the reality that we are living in.

Sometimes we mistake the activities of our body and mind for the essence of aliveness. Because we've never experienced life without them, we tend to associate the feeling of being alive with the actions of our body and mind. We eat, sleep, think, walk, and dream with the help of our body, so it's easy to confuse these activities with the experience of being alive. However, what we're truly searching for is the pure essence of aliveness, unburdened by the distractions and limitations of the mind and body. This is the true nature of our being, and it is what we long to reconnect with in life.

You have always assumed that your body is the source of your aliveness. However, just close your eyes for a moment and ask yourself this question: What if reality is different? What if your aliveness is not a product of your body, but the source of it? The question of aliveness has plagued us since the beginning of time, and the answer to it is what we have been searching for.

To assume that the body is the origin of consciousness and aliveness is illogical. How can something as physical and mechanical as the body give rise to something as intricate and enigmatic as consciousness? How can something as tangible and material as the body give rise to something as intangible and ethereal as aliveness? This is the question that has driven the search for answers across various fields, including religion, philosophy, science, and spirituality. However, what many fail to realize is that aliveness itself is the source and origin of everything, and this search for answers has been, in a sense, an exploration of our own essence.

The ultimate reality is your pure, untainted Self, which transcends all qualities and attributes. We attribute qualities such as size, subtlety, beauty, materiality, and spirituality to existence, but these are all human constructions. Existence itself is beyond these qualities and is a transcendent phenomenon that cannot be grasped by our senses. The pure essence of aliveness, the Self, and consciousness cannot be comprehended, but it can be realized within, and that is the goal of the spiritual seeker. Finding your True Self is about realizing it within yourself. When you experience that you are the source of your life and everything that happens in it, a new sense of certainty will emerge. What is missing in life is this certainty - the certainty of knowing your True Self.

This pure state of being, devoid of all the qualities and characteristics of life, is what Buddha referred to as 'Nirvana' or 'Emptiness'. 'Nirvana' symbolizes ultimate freedom, a state of complete 'Emptiness'. In this state, one transcends the limitations of the body and mind, and experiences a deep awakening to one's true Self. However, the concept of 'Nothingness' in Buddhism has often been misconstrued as a state devoid of all experiences. People often question how 'Nothingness' could be the ultimate goal of a human life, and how it can be equivalent to Enlightenment, which is supposed to be a state of profound realization.

Very few people truly understand the concept of "Nothingness." No other enlightened being has described the state of spiritual enlightenment better than Buddha. Enlightenment is not an experience, but rather a realization of one's true self. People often describe it as an experience and attach human qualities to it. However, Buddha's concept of "Nothingness" is accurate as it does not describe enlightenment as a human experience, but rather as the end of all experiences and familiarity with life. At the moment of awakening, everything one is and knows comes to an end, leaving nothing to experience but pure nothingness.

The answer lies in the realization that there is a presence beyond the mind and body that is aware of "Nothingness". It is this presence, which is your true self, that is capable of experiencing the state of "Nothingness". The fact that one can even contemplate the concept of "Nothingness" is proof of the presence of the Self. The mind and body are limited to experiences and perceptions, but the true self transcends beyond these limitations and is capable of experiencing the state of "Nothingness". This realization is the essence of spiritual enlightenment.

Your ultimate goal in meditation is to discover the pure and pristine observer within you. As long as you are tied to the experiences of your mind and body, you will not be able to find this observer. When you perceive reality through your mind and body, you are limited to the experiences that are programmed into you. Meditation is a process of undoing these programming patterns and transcending beyond your conditioning to reach this pure state of perception. By letting go of your attachment to your mind and body and simply being present, you will experience reality in a completely new way.

This new way of perceiving will let you see things without the biases and prejudices of your conditioned mind for the first time. There is a beautiful phrase in Sanskrit called "Aham Brahmasmi" which means "I am God" or "I am the Creator". The difference between the Creator and you is only a matter of attachment. Since you are attached to your mind and body, you create things that are limited to your mind and body. "Aham Brahmasmi" means that the Creator is not somewhere outside, but instead, he is within you and he is you.

The path to finding your True Self involves the practice of meditation. Meditation helps in gradually releasing deep-rooted attachments to the mind and body, leading to a state of transcendental reality. It is a simple yet effective way to go beyond conditioning and find the ultimate solution to life's problems.

Initially, meditation can feel like a battle with the mind, as it is filled with constant distractions and disturbances. At this stage, it is important to overcome the constant chatter of the mind in order to find a quiet inner space. This can be a challenging phase, but with persistence, it is possible to achieve mastery over the mind.

Who wins this battle, you or your mind, determines your progress in meditation. If the mind prevails, you may struggle with staying focused and finding deeper meaning. But if you are successful in controlling your mind, you can move on to the higher stages of meditation - experiencing it through the body. True meditation occurs when it becomes an embodied experience, not just a mental one. While gaining control over the mind can bring relaxation and happiness, it is only through the body that you can experience true transcendental bliss and enlightenment.

The objective of meditation is to move beyond the sensory experiences of the mind and body and reach a state of inner stillness and quietness. This state is characterized by the absence of all sensory experiences, including noise, movement, pain, smell, taste, sight, and touch. By focusing on one of these senses and gradually moving towards its empty zone, you can gradually quiet your mind and body, and experience a deep sense of inner peace and serenity.

For example, you can start with the visual sense. You can begin your meditation by focusing on an object, let's say a candle flame. The aim of your meditation is to maintain focus on the candle flame and find the internal zone of emptiness where there is no image.

Similarly, you can do this with sound. You can listen to some soothing instrumental music and strive to find a moment of complete internal silence. In theory, meditation is one of the simplest things you can do. All you have to do is go beyond the object of perception and find its empty zone. However, you will soon realize the actual difficulty when you start practicing. Your mind will present the biggest challenge to meditation. After just a few months of trying, you may conclude that your mind has a mind of its own. Controlling your ever-active mind will be your greatest challenge in life.

The ultimate goal of meditation is to reach a state of "Nothingness", where there is nothing left to watch. This requires going beyond the comfortable body, and even questioning our habits and beliefs about sitting, closing our eyes, and breathing. The journey towards Enlightenment is not complete until we reach this state of pure awareness and "Nothingness".

The spiritual journey is a process of letting go of everything that is not you. As you continue to watch the sensations of your body and find the empty zone within, you will gradually start to understand the true nature of your existence. The closer you get to your True Self, the less you will be affected by the material world, and the more you will experience inner peace and happiness.

This journey is not easy, but it is worth every step. Meditation is a tool that will help you get there, but it is not the only way. You can also find your True Self through service, devotion, and self-reflection. Whatever path you choose, always remember that the journey is just as important as the destination. As you travel, you will learn new things about yourself and the world, and you will grow as a person. So, it's important to be patient, be persistent, and enjoy the journey.

Meditation is not just about knowing more about it, but about having a direct experience of reality. It is a process of self-discovery and not just a collection of concepts and ideas. While intellectual questioning can help guide you on your path, it should not become the focus of your meditation practice.

The ultimate goal is to transcend the mind and experience reality beyond concepts and language. So, it is important to keep a balance between understanding and direct experience, and to let go of any preconceived notions and biases as you continue to delve deeper into the practice of meditation.

A technique to help detach from the attachment to the mind and body is through negation. By constantly questioning, you can begin to disassociate from everything you believe to be true about yourself. A teacher might ask a student questions about the nature of reality, consciousness, and Truth, and respond with "No" to every answer the student gives, such as "Is it the mind?", "No, it's not the mind". This process of negation is meant to strip away every concept and construct that you have created for yourself. Once all of these are negated, you may have a moment of realization where you recognize that even when everything is gone, you still exist. This realization can lead to a greater understanding of the true nature of the Self and the Truth you have been seeking all your life.

Just think about the magnitude of the moment when you realize that the truth you've been searching for all your life is yourself. You don't need to go anywhere to find it, it's always been right here in the present moment. By constantly moving, searching, and wandering, you were actually distracting yourself from the truth. Your quest for answers was leading you further away from yourself, and your path was blocking you from the truth. However, this does not mean that you can reach your true self without seeking. The confusion about whether to seek or not arises from the limitations of language. When you meditate, you are clearly seeking something, such as relaxation, inner peace, happiness, or something else. But the very act of seeking can prevent you from achieving that state. The key is to learn when to seek and when to let go, and this will come with practice.

You need to keep searching until you fully realize the significance of your true identity. Often, you are lost in a mental construct of life and not fully present in the experience of life happening within and around you. By intentionally observing the experiences occurring in the present moment, you can gradually begin to truly experience them. This realization will lead you to question, "If this central entity of experiencing does not exist, if I do not exist, then what is the meaning of all the things happening around me?" The deeper you delve into this understanding, the sooner you will recognize that without your presence, none of the things happening around you can be experienced. You must be there to experience heat and cold, light and darkness, as these sensations cannot exist by themselves.

If fundamental realities of existence, such as heat and cold, or light and darkness, cannot exist independently, then what can exist independently? This realization leads us to understand that our experiencing self is the most important aspect of existence and that we are at the center of life, and indeed, life itself. Existence cannot make sense without us, and we have missed this realization because we have always looked at our life from an external perspective. However, once we learn to look at everything from an internal perspective, existence will make perfect sense, and our lives will make perfect sense as well.

ENLIGHTENMENT

"Your own Self-Realization is the greatest service you can render the world."

Ramana Maharshi

Why do people use these different terms: Awakened, Enlightened, or Self-Realization? You've said they all mean the same thing, so why isn't there just one word?

Enlightenment is a unique and profound experience that is difficult to define or describe with a single definition or explanation. It cannot be compared to any other worldly experience, as it transcends the limitations of human language and the external world. The experience of awakening is personal and unique, and can only be fully understood by the individual who experiences it.

Awakening is a distinct experience that occurs when you surpass the limitations of your mind and body and reach a state of transcendental reality. It is called Enlightenment because it is a moment of clarity and understanding in which the entire universe becomes illuminated. Until then, you have been living in ignorance or darkness. Enlightenment signifies that you have emerged from the darkness and entered into the light. This experience is also known as Self-Realization because it is the first time you understand the independent and transcendental nature of your true Self. Before this realization, you may have identified yourself with your mind and body, but now you comprehend the magnificent and true essence of your Self.

Buddha called the ultimate experience, "Nirvana." Nirvana means "an absolute merging into the ultimate." There is no English equivalent for the word Nirvana, but if you do a literal translation, it translates to "extinguishing, extinction, or absolute annihilation." Despite its definition, Nirvana has a much more positive connotation. It represents a merging, a sense of becoming one with everything. You can also describe it as "the experience of nothingness," as it is a moment when you have no thoughts and are not aware of your body. Regardless of the name, the experience remains the same.

Enlightenment is a unique moment of absolute awareness, when your mind is at rest, and you are completely awake. It is a moment of total relaxation, and freedom from all desires, even the desire for enlightenment itself. This experience is unique and one that you may have had before, without even realizing it. As you currently identify yourself solely with your physical body, this experience can be hard to understand. Enlightenment is that moment when you temporarily detach from your body and glimpse the transcendental nature of your true Self.

There is no experience like Enlightenment. It completely transforms your perception and understanding of life. Everything will change in a beautiful way once you become Enlightened. You will understand that you have a body, but you are not the body. This is the most significant change that occurs. We have not learned to contemplate life independently from the body. All our inquiries and investigations of life have been conducted through the body without a direct perception of life.

Your body, by its very nature of perception, divides everything. It is your mind that fills in the gaps, using information from previous experiences, to give you a perception of completeness. When you look at a tree, your mind won't tell you, "You're only seeing half the tree." It will fill in the other half, using your past experiences and imagination. Physically, we can only see a part of the tree, while the rest is imagined by our mind. Everything we perceive is partial and incomplete, which is why we do not truly know what life is in its entirety. Life is a whole and cannot be grasped in bits and pieces. We can either understand life completely or not at all.

After your Enlightenment, you will be able to see the tree in its entirety. You don't have to be physically near the tree to experience this. When you awaken, you will become intimately familiar with all things, such as trees, birds, insects, clouds, the sky, and more. When you step outside after your realization, you will notice a difference in your perception of the world. For the first time, you will see things from an inside-out perspective. You will no longer just see the tree as a collection of leaves, wood, and bark, but instead, you will understand the life that flows through it. You will understand that just as you are experiencing life as an individual being, the tree is also experiencing life as a separate being, albeit in a very different way.

The significant difference between you and everything else is your awareness of your own existence. While animals and plants possess physical bodies, they lack the self-awareness of their own existence. Most people also live their lives without much contemplation of their true identity, growing up in a highly conditioned society and going through life without examining their own existence. However, the pursuit of spirituality, self-discovery, and Enlightenment marks the beginning of a conscious evolution. Choosing to move beyond mere animalistic existence and exploring the nature of reality within and around us is the beginning of a spiritual journey.

In our human experience, spirituality is the only conscious evolution that we can choose to embark upon. Other aspects of life, such as living, growing, having children, aging, and dying, happen to us regardless of our awareness or involvement. Life is more of a happening than a doing. Even in moments when we believe we are making choices, we often fail to recognize that there are countless factors beyond our control that shape our decisions. The idea of choice may be more of an illusion than we realize. We rarely stop to observe this phenomenon, instead preferring to believe that we are in control of our lives, as it gives us a sense of purpose and hope. But, if we are honest with ourselves, we must admit that almost everything that has happened in our lives has simply happened, and we have had little control over it.

If we have so little control over our lives, then what is it that we can actually choose? What separates us from everything else in existence? What makes us special? The answer is simple: the only thing we can choose in life is a conscious evolution. The moment we decide to become aware of everything happening in our lives, we begin to grow spiritually. Choosing to consciously evolve is the only power we have.

Why is it that very few people know about and pursue Self-Realization, although it is the highest goal of a human life?

Survival is a basic necessity of human life, and it involves acquiring knowledge about people, the environment, the past, the future, and many other things. Only after fulfilling this basic necessity can we turn our attention to higher knowledge, such as Self-Realization. Self-Realization is not a basic necessity of life; it is the highest potential of life. Only those who are able to look beyond their basic needs can pursue spirituality. There is another reason why Self-Realization is known to only a few people, and that is purely a social factor.

In order to function, society requires the collective efforts of many individuals. Education systems have been created to ensure that future generations have a basic understanding of human society and are able to contribute to it. However, the focus of formal education is not on personal growth or Self-Realization, as it is viewed as an impractical or irrelevant goal for society at large. Society is based on principles of cooperation, knowledge sharing, and uniformity, while Self-Realization is a personal journey to discover one's highest potential. Without conscious effort, individuals can easily overlook the tremendous possibilities of spiritual growth and Self-Realization.

Society is a complex machine with its own goals and objectives. Unless we make a conscious effort to pursue our own individual paths, we can easily get caught up in following society's dreams and desires. Spiritual growth is a personal choice, and it requires us to resist societal pressures to some extent. It's not advisable to go completely against societal norms as we would lose out on the benefits that come from being part of the collective. Instead, finding a middle ground between meeting our material needs and advancing in our spiritual growth is the key to living a fulfilling life.

It's important to strike a balance between materialism and spirituality, as becoming too materialistic can make you miss the beauty of Self-Realization, while being overly spiritual could make you miss out on the conveniences of modern life. Your intelligence aids in finding the right balance between the two. Society may not encourage the pursuit of spirituality, but as an individual, it's essential to resist the pressure and move towards your highest self. It takes courage to walk the silent path.

ABOUT THE AUTHOR:

Avi's extraordinary understanding of life comes from his experiential journey into the depths of meditation. His teachings are aimed at helping individuals find their true selves.

Avi believes that the ultimate purpose of an individual's life is to realize the Truth that hides within. All his books, teachings, and programs are directed toward this cause. He is a teacher, friend, and above all, a beautiful human being guiding individuals on the path of Self-Realization.

"Nirvana" is a non-profit spiritual organization helping individuals explore and understand the mystical teachings of enlightened teachers of the world.

Visit www.nirvana.foundation to know more about Avi and his vision. We would also appreciate if you can take some time to leave your review of the book on Amazon.

Made in the USA
Las Vegas, NV
15 September 2023